Tanzania's Land Rush

Tanzania's Land Rush

Impacts of the Farmland Investment Game

Joanny Bélair

ZED

LONDON • NEW YORK • OXFORD • NEW DELHI • SYDNEY

ZED BOOKS
Bloomsbury Publishing Plc
50 Bedford Square, London, WC1B 3DP, UK
1385 Broadway, New York, NY 10018, USA
29 Earlsfort Terrace, Dublin 2, Ireland

BLOOMSBURY and Zed Books are trademarks of Bloomsbury Publishing Plc

First published in Great Britain, 2023
This paperback edition published in 2024

Series design by Adriana Brioso
Cover image: Onion farming in the Eyasi area, Tanzania.
(© EmmePi Images/Alamy Stock Photo)

A catalogue record for this book is available from the British Library.

A catalog record for this book is available from the Library of Congress.

ISBN: HB: 978-1-3502-7390-0
        PB: 978-1-3502-7393-1
        ePDF: 978-1-3502-7392-4
        eBook: 978-1-3502-7391-7

Typeset by Integra Software Services Pvt. Ltd.

To find out more about our authors and books visit www.bloomsbury.com
and sign up for our newsletters.

Contents

Illustrations

Figures

Table

Preface

This book is the result of my PhD research project and is an adaptation of my dissertation that I successfully defended at the University of Ottawa, Canada, in 2019 (Bélair, 2019). Undertaking such a research project has been challenging on so many levels and I want to emphasize that researching the local impacts associated with new farmland investments is politically contentious in Tanzania. As a result, my fieldwork for this research was difficult because my efforts to uncover hidden political dynamics were at best perceived by some informants as annoying, sometimes upsetting; at worse they were perceived as threatening their very interests associated with these investment projects. In addition, the fact that I adopted ethnography as a method involved important ethical, and pragmatic considerations that affected my research process and my findings. Reflexivity was key as I was continuously and as transparently as possible assessing my position in the field and its impact on my research process and findings (Irwin, 2006; Jean Wood, 2007; Berger, 2015; Deane and Stevano, 2016). To transparently assess the limits of this book and to also warn researchers that are interested in researching similar issues, I think five specific points are worth developing on.

First, there was this challenge of rendering the field legible to me. Although Scott (1998) primarily develops the concept of 'legibility' to discuss the capacity of the state 'to see and read', his concept greatly captures as well the reality of a junior researcher starting his fieldwork in a foreign country. Indeed, increasing the legibility of the field was an important challenge for me throughout my fieldwork. A trivial example that illustrates this is the inexistence of maps in most rural areas of Tanzania. Maps, boundaries and roads are all part of local knowledge. Orientation between villages, boundaries and mapping the investment in relation to villages surrounding it were all tiny challenges associated with increasing my capacity at better seeing and reading the local context. For example, the map of the investments you will find in Chapter 5: p. 66 is not coming from any government authorities, as they do not have such cartographical overview of the district investment projects (at least to my knowledge). Rather, this Rufiji map is the result of my observations, my fieldnotes on the distance and roads, the approximate plans I made to map the district and its various investment projects. It then became legible and geographically accurate, thanks to an expert I commissioned. Another example is my initially limited understanding of some key political notions in the Tanzanian context. Concepts such as consultation, agreement and democracy were at first framed by my Western conceptual framework, and this Western framing influenced my reading of some social situations. It takes time to question my own unacknowledged assumptions about meaning, and it has an impact on how I conducted my first interviews. This could have led to important biases if left unchallenged. The same is true, and perhaps even more important, in relation to actors' interactions with each other, and with me. The normative structure regulating social interactions differs from one country to another. Reading people reactions; contextualizing their interactions; understanding the hidden signification of expressions, words, and ways of behaving is part of a time-consuming learning process. In practice, as I became increasingly aware, what sometimes appeared to me as petty details might prove of paramount importance to my informants. For instance, in most Tanzanian rural communities, I had to introduce myself and clarified why I was there. It is a way to secure both access to informants and my safety during the research process. Failing to do so may have important consequences, and could even threaten your life. For instance, the whole country was shocked in October 2016 when three Tanzanian researchers were brutally attacked by a group of villagers near Dodoma. They were slashed with axes and machetes before being burned in their car (Ubwani, 2016). After investigation, the police discovered that the attack was triggered by these villagers' belief that the researchers were 'witches'. They failed to introduce themselves to village leaders, thereby leaving room for ontological uncertainty and ambiguity about their intentions and motives.

Second, preserving my independence was constantly part of my preoccupations. Getting access to marginalized communities is a complicated matter. Several small details might influence how I was perceived, and more importantly, what story informants choose to tell me. To give a concrete example, arriving by car in a Tanzanian village is often the first clue that the community will use to determine your socio-political status. In the most remote communities, it is common for villagers to associate cars with government's agents. If the community reads you as being with the Tanzanian government, gaining villagers' trust becomes almost impossible. Similarly, being introduced to the local population through local elites is likely to provoke both mistrust and fear towards me, as potential retaliation from the politically powerful may be very threatening to local people. Local elites may even use this as a strategy to surreptitiously discredit me especially if they are trying to conceal information. Therefore, as Cramer et al. (2016) contend, the risk of losing independence is tangible for the researcher inattentive to the fact that the opposition of elites to independent research may affect his access to the subordinate class. Concretely, it could have limited my access to villagers which would have been very problematic because my research focus was on how local dynamics were impacted by new farmland investments. One way my research assistant and I found to mitigate this was to always introduce ourselves and our research project to the leaders of a given village first. We informed them about our intention to conduct interviews with villagers, but always remained very vague about the 'when'. Waiting a couple of days or even weeks before coming back to conduct the interviews with villagers often secured our independence from leaders who would have otherwise insisted on accompanying us in the village. In addition, we adopted the villagers' main mode of transportation to move around: walking. People were sometimes very surprised to see a *mzungu* – a foreigner of European/American descent – walking through the bush under a burning sun to speak to them. They were used to seeing wealthy *mzungu* moving around in cars, be they investors or tourists. I believe it may have changed their perception of who I was and helped me somehow to gain their trust. Moreover, walking bore other advantages as I often met interesting people along the way, and got a better understanding of villagers' day-to-day reality.

Third, another very crucial challenge associated with the legibility of the field for a researcher relates to his own safety. Sometimes, misinterpreting informants' reactions has put me in real danger. For example, once, in Rufiji district, I spoke with district officials to get information about one specific investor. I wanted to visit the investment site, but these officials were very reluctant to let me, even though they never said so directly. Everything became a complicated matter. We argued, discussed and finally I complied with some of their demands. For instance, I hired their motorbike drivers at an exorbitant price to get their approval. In the end, after a rather long negotiating process, we left and went to the investment site. My initial assumption was that they did not want us to visit the farm because they wanted to hide the investor's lack of commitment to operationalize his investment. That proved only partly true. Later, I found out that this specific investor was in a conflict with the administrators of the Selous Game Reserve, with which his farmland has shared boundaries. The land he acquired through his clientelistic networks was reserved land, which created a legal problem between district and National Park authorities. The conflict had escalated, and at the moment of my visit to his farm, the Selous Game Reserve guards had been instructed to shoot anyone seen on the land located near the Park's borders. Concretely then, by visiting this specific investment site, we were putting ourselves in danger of getting shot, without even being aware of the risk. This whole episode made me realize two crucial things. First, the political game at play is sometimes bigger than what I can anticipate as a foreign researcher. Second, for those district officials, hiding this contentious conflict was more valuable than ensuring my safety. Consequently, the fact that elites may manipulate information for a variety of reasons implied not only the risks of losing my independence and having my results biased by their interests, but also tangible risks to my safety. Furthermore, safety risks were substantial not only for me, but also for my informants. Tanzania is still an authoritarian state. As will be discussed in Chapter 4, since Magufuli came into power in late October 2015, authoritarian tendencies have been increasing: detention of opposition leaders, banning of public demonstrations, policy changes in media regulations, increased control of social media, numerous uninvestigated cases of people speaking against the government who have disappeared or have been arrested, etc. Political violence was an issue at the time of my fieldwork. Corruption is also widespread, rule of law is problematic and for many Tanzanians, defending their rights is a tricky matter, which requires financial and political capital that most of them do not have. In this context, I soon realized the importance of the question of informed consent. This created an important and constant ethical dilemma for me during my whole fieldwork: How to conduct independent research and gather the views of marginalized farmers while at the same time ensuring my own and my informants' safety? In some cases, people agreed to speak with me about some very political issues. I protected their anonymity and the confidentiality of the information they trusted me with. However, it is undisputable that many informants also remained silent about some of the most pressing issues for fear of political retaliation and violence. Thus, it is not easy to assess which story I had access to, or what is missing from it even if I triangulated information. It is important to acknowledge that my findings are limited somewhat by the impacts of the political context prevailing at the time of my fieldwork, and all its underlying implications on relations of power, on people perceptions, on what they dared denounce or speak about and what they did not.

Fourth, my positionality and the relations of power it involved have marked all my interactions with my informants as well as my research process and findings. Even though I did not intend to, I reproduced relations of power throughout my fieldwork. I am a Western, young, white and educated woman. I have options that are not available to most people I met and interviewed. The most obvious of these is that I can travel to Tanzania to study these investment projects, entering and leaving the country as I please. My power position was thus inaccessible for most of my informants, including government officials. How then do we assess this impact on the relationship the researcher developed with her informants? How did all these power inequalities shape their expectations, their answers, their very interactions with me? They do indeed have critical consequences. Assessing them though is complex. On the one hand, I do believe that my informants were speaking more freely with me because they were conscious, as I came to be, of my position as a foreigner to the field of study. My very position gave me a status independent of the clientelistic and political networks that regulate their social life. My perceived independence provided them with an opportunity to voice their concerns more freely. Being listened to was thus an important unanticipated benefit of their participation in my research. Yet, at the same time, I created expectations that were impossible for me to meet. For instance, I realized that my listening and my very presence and interest in those land issues gave local communities hope that things would change. They were expecting me to raise awareness about the most pressing issues they were facing, i.e. land dispossession, land issues, land conflicts, violence, indebtment, social inequalities, etc. Many overestimated both my political powers and my commitment to get politically engaged in those issues. Often, I felt as much powerless as they do, in the face of predatory, clientelistic and sometimes violent practices. However, it is true that my position as a *mzungu* gave me privileged access to key actors, to government officials and to information. There is an informal law of secrecy surrounding most farmland investments I have been investigating in Tanzania. At one point, continuously interviewing different actors, at various levels, and triangulating information bore fruit. For instance, in Rufiji district, by gathering, using and cross-checking villages' maps with the information provided by the Tanzanian Investment Centre and investors, I succeeded in mapping all ongoing investment projects. Yet the fact that I am white and thus very visible in rural Tanzanian settings also made things more difficult. Sometimes, I walked in the bush several hours to avoid local and district officials controlling my access to informants.

Fifth, unequal access to information affected my research object, even involuntarily. For example, in some instances, my questions about investment projects put me in a position where local communities knew less about what was going on than I did. This was the case in a small village I researched. The chairman of this village in collusion with some local leaders had agreed to sell the village land to an investor, without consulting or securing the consent of the villagers. As a result, villagers were unaware of the deal. This created an important ethical dilemma for me. Rightly, villagers started asking me questions. After all, I was there to investigate the impacts of an investor who had acquired their land without them knowing it. They quickly understood that this would lead to their displacement by government officials, dispossessing them at the same time from their rights to this land. The matter was even more delicate because I knew that this specific farmland project was not tentative. It had already been approved by the Ministry of Land and was currently being reviewed by the President himself. In this context, how much information should I share? How is my information-sharing impacting the course of events? How do I assess this impact on my research object? Those are important and thorny questions. I must acknowledge that my presence had an impact in the field and on the very object I studied and that it is impossible to fully measure the scope of that impact. It is inevitable, and a constitutive part of my research process.

Research is subjective, knowledge-building is interactive and there might be unexpected consequences to our purposeful actions. In the interest of transparency, however, I want to clarify my standpoint when such situations occurred. I chose to always share information with affected communities. Probably, my presence in the field led to villagers being more informed about new investment projects, and about their land rights, and possibly, led them to subsequently challenge their local leaders on these issues.

While bearing these thoughts in mind, I want to conclude by emphasizing that one important concern that has stayed with me since I came back from my fieldwork in 2017 was how to make my findings more visible outside academia. How to ensure that the Tanzanians that have entrusted me with their life stories, their problems, their hopes and their grievances will get their voices heard? How to make sure that this is not only a PhD dissertation that will lie in a library, only being read by a few scholars interested in the field? How can I be fair towards my informants? I felt an important need of denouncing the many inequities I have witnessed, the wrongs, the unfairness. I also felt that it was important to share the lessons I have learned with development practitioners, development agencies and donors. To speak up, to engage a conversation on those issues with the hope that perhaps, some of my findings might reveal useful to do better. This is what this book is also about.

Acknowledgements

When I first started this research project, I would not have guessed how transforming it would be personally and intellectually. I am indebted to so many people that have supported me, on so many different levels, on the rather long journey that led to that book. I want first to thank Cédric Jourde, my PhD thesis director. Cédric has introduced me to African politics, and has influenced my thinking and guided me since my postgraduate studies. It is definitely because of his moral and intellectual support that I can now say that this book is finally published. Without him, I do believe this book would not have been possible, even if he would disagree. His sharp brain, his patience, his humanity, his open mind and so on. Many thanks, many thanks Cédric.

Also, this research would not have been possible without Godwin, my research assistant in Tanzania. We travelled the whole country together and we faced all kind of situations. We walked the bush searching for herders, we avoided the suspicions of district officials, we hired motorbike drivers to drive us around, we went looking for missing villages, we sat to speak with so many villagers, etc. Without his support, his acuteness, his sensitivity to this research project and aim, I do believe that I would not have been able to make complete sense of these findings, to interview so many people, and, more basically, to survive on a personal level in those very rural Tanzanian settings.

Moreover, I want to thank Mehdi Benhessou. His listening, his patience, his encouragements and his love made it possible for me to undertake this book project. Other friends have also been invaluable while I was becoming a bit obsessed with this whole research project and they have provided me feedback that has helped me to deepen my reflection and get through, namely Michael Nolet, Johan Hosselaer, Darren Brazeau, David Kroeker Maus, Julian Tadesse, France Poulin and Nas. I also want to express my gratitude to the many people in Tanzania who have agreed to share their stories with me. Lastly, I am indebted to so many colleagues for numerous interesting discussions, comments and research suggestions. In particular, I want to thank Philippe

Martin, Stéphanie Bacher, Thabit Jacob, Lars Buur, Rasmus Pedersen, Howard Stein, Malin Nystrand, Marie Gagné, Derek Hall, Linda Engström, Masalu Luhula, Emmanuel Sulle, Nisha Shah, Luc Turgeon, Mark Salter, Guus van Westen, Gemma van der Haar, Annelies Zoomers. I sincerely hope I am not forgetting anyone.

Abbreviations

ASP	Afro-Shirazi Party
BRN	Big Results Now
CAS	Contingencies, Agency and Structure
CCM	*Chama Cha Mapinduzi*
Chadema	*Chama cha Maendeleo na Demokrasia*
CCRO	Certificate of Customary Rights of Occupancy
DC	District Commissioner
DED	District Executive Director
DPP	Director of Public Prosecutions
FAO	Food and Agriculture Organization
FDI	Foreign Direct Investments
IFAD	International Fund for Agricultural Development
IMF	International Monetary Fund
ITR	The Individualization, Titling and Registration
LIU	Land Investment Unit
LRRRI	Land Rights research and Resources institute
MKUKUTA	Tanzania's National Strategy for Growth and Reduction of Poverty
MP	Member of Parliament
NAP	National Agriculture Policy

NARCO	National Ranching Company
NORAD	Norwegian Agency for Development Cooperation
NESP	National Economic Survival Program
New Alliance	New Alliance for Food Security and Nutrition Initiative
NFYDP	National Five-Year Development Plan
NGO	Non-governmental Organization
NLP	National Land Policy
PPCB	Prevention and Combating of Corruption Bureau
PPSL	Program for Planning, Surveying, and Land Titling in Tanzania
PRAI	Principles of Responsible Agricultural Investment
RAI	Principles for Responsible Investments in Agriculture and Food Systems
RUBADA	Rufiji Basin Development Authority
SAGCOT	Southern Agricultural Growth Corridor
SSA	Sub-Saharan Africa
TANESCO	Tanzania Electric Supply Company
TANU	Tanganyika African National Union
TIB	Development Bank of Tanzania
TIC	Tanzanian Investment Center
TRA	Tanzania Revenue Authority
UKAWA	Opposition Coalition
UNCTAD	UN Conference on Trade and Development
VA	Village Assembly

VEO	Village Executive Officer
VC	Village Council
VLUP	Village Land Use Plan
WB	World Bank

Tanzania map with regions and districts

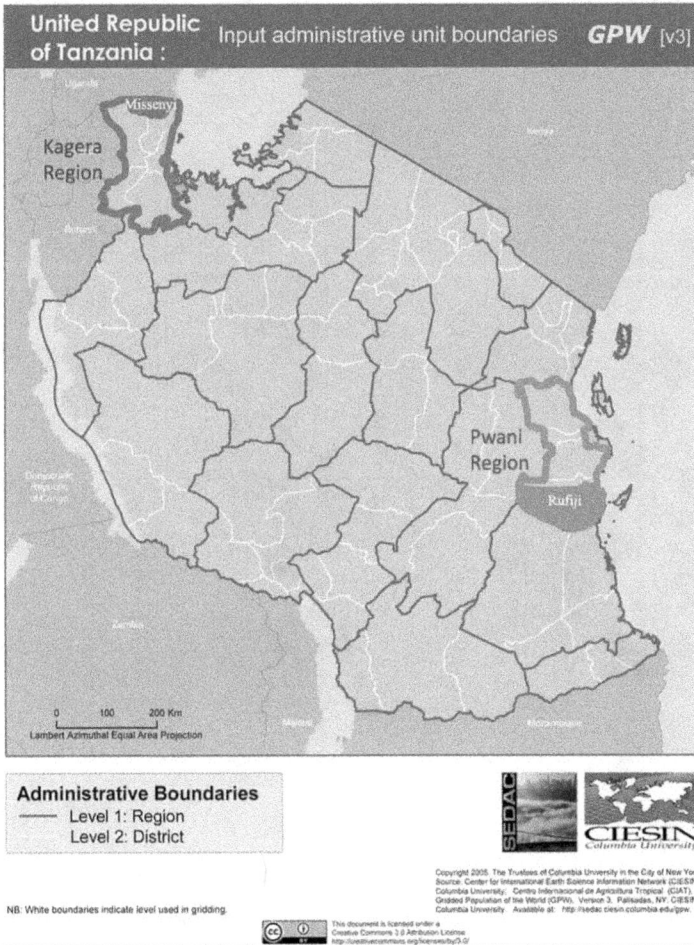

Figure 1 Map of Tanzania. Copyright 2005. The Trustees of Columbia University in the City of New York

1

Introduction

Since the global energy, food and economic crises of 2008, investors' rising interest in farmland in developing countries, or the so-called land grabbing phenomenon has gained sustained attention in scholarly and international development circles. According to the International Land Coalition, between 2008 and 2012, the documented land transactions could represent as much as 1.7 per cent of the global agricultural area (Anseeuw et al., 2012). Although figures diverge, and their validity has been questioned, these land transactions are undeniably significant and may restructure the global agricultural landscape (HLPE, 2011; Margulis, McKeon and Borras Jr, 2013, 2; Clapp, 2014). Africa has been the continent most affected by these new investments. The phenomenon is symbolic of increased land commodification and agricultural financialization: investors' renewed interest in farmland has been linked to its attractiveness as a safe and lucrative financial asset in times of increasing global uncertainties. This land rush has also been directly associated to global narratives on agricultural modernization and development through foreign direct investments (FDI) on 'cheap, unproductive and/or idle' farmland. Since most people live in rural areas and survive on subsistence farming in sub-Saharan Africa (SSA), international institutions, investors and donors portray agricultural development as the most promising sector to favour economic growth and poverty reduction (Deininger and Byerlee, 2011). The expectation is that investors, by undertaking commercial agricultural ventures in developing countries, will favour productivity increase by 'bridging the yield gap between current and potential production on land identified as marginal' (McMichael, 2014, p. 35). Many African states are also playing an important role in welcoming these new investors. For example, in Tanzania, the government has been actively courting them, arguing that they will ensure agriculture's modernization and economic development. From 2005 to 2009, about four million hectares were requested for land transactions (Sulle and Nelson, 2009).

Yet, despite the hype, since 2012, within SSA, farmland acquisitions have slowed down and most projects have faced important operational difficulties, leading to their cancellation or abandonment. Indeed, as many scholars have observed, the implementation gap is substantial (Woertz, 2013, p. 90; Feintrenie, 2014; Keene et al., 2015; Visser, 2015; Nolte, Chamberlain and Giger, 2016) and failure is a common outcome associated with this land rush (Spoor, 2012; Visser, Mamonova and Spoor, 2012; Bräutigam and Zhang, 2013; Anseeuw and Boche, 2015; Goetz, 2015; Hopma, 2015; Gill, 2016; Magnan and Sunley, 2017). For instance, a 2018 GRAIN report documents a total of 135 flopped farmland deals during the period between 2007 and 2017 which represents 17.5 million hectares (GRAIN, 2018, p. 2). Biofuel investments have the highest failure rates: for the confirmed deals, 85 per cent of investors had ceased operations (Antonelli et al., 2015; Di Matteo and Schoneveld, 2016, p. 20; see also Ahmed, Campion and Gasparatos, 2017). For agricultural investments, the failure rate is smaller but still significant. In their review of 482 approved investments between 2002 and 2013, Di Matteo and Schoneveld (2016) found that 23.6 per cent have been cancelled or abandoned. Importantly though, peasants rarely gain back their land rights, even when the investment project proves a failure. Land dispossession appears thus to be a lasting outcome of this land rush.

Regarding the successful farmland investments – operational even if scaled-back, local impacts also tend to fall short of expectations. For instance, employment creation seems to be usually a short-term effect with limited evidence of lasting economic impacts. Newly created jobs are usually seasonal, low-qualified and temporary (Schoneveld, German and Nutakor, 2010; Murray Li, 2011; Alhassan, Shaibu and Kuwornu, 2018; Bluwstein et al., 2018; Ayelazuno, 2019). Although some studies show that farmland investments created socio-economic benefits, such as employment, increased access to inputs and technology, and income generation (e.g. Brüntrup et al., 2016; Herrmann, 2017), those benefits are often unevenly distributed at the local level. For example, Porsani et al. (2019) report that the company recruited only what they considered local 'progressive' farmers for their Mozambican project, i.e. the farmers who already were the wealthier of the community, with bigger parcels of land, and more likely to use inputs and irrigation systems. Boamah's (2014) analysis of a Canadian project in Ghana claims that the ability of locals to be included in the project was heavily influenced by the actors' lobbying capacity and their influence in the community. Even the so-called inclusive investments, such as contract farming schemes, tend to consolidate already existing social differentiation dynamics, leading to the exclusion of the poorest at the expense of the wealthiest or local elites (Herrmann, 2017; Lanz, Gerber and Haller, 2018; Kansanga and Luginaah, 2019; Porsani, Caretta and Lehtilä, 2019; Vercillo and Hird-Younger, 2019; Abate, 2020). In particular, marginal groups such as migrants and women tend to be more negatively affected (Baumgartner et al., 2015; Boamah and Overå, 2016; Brüntrup et al., 2018; Osabuohien et al., 2019). Therefore, although this land rush induced socio-economic transformative processes at the local level, we should be careful with the claim that those new investments alleviate poverty and foster socio-economic development. Not all actors are equal in their possibilities and capacity to benefit from them. Many studies show that new farmland investments tend to reinforce pre-existing social and economic inequalities (Boamah and Overå, 2016; see also Jayne et al., 2019).

What explains these dominant trends? Why are so many of those investments, operational or not, failing to bring sustainable and lasting local development? How can we better capture and understand their local impacts? Using Tanzania as a case-study, this book tackles those questions and argues that we need a relational and political analysis to capture and understand the local effects of this land rush. First, acknowledging the complexity, the fluidity and the dynamism of agrarian systems in developing countries, and the socio-political and relational context in which they are embedded is key (Akram-Lodhi and Kay, 2010; White et al., 2012; Hall, 2013; Brent, 2015). Indeed, global capitalism is not straightforwardly restructuring developing countries' local agrarian contexts. Seeing African governments, political elites and peasants as either passive victims of global market forces or as actively resisting them is misleading. They do participate in and negotiate the transformation of their political economy induced by this global land rush: adopting their own narratives, transforming, or creating new policies, inducing structural changes and institutional transformations. Second, processes of farmland commodification led to the creation of new sites of economic accumulation, to which certain economic and political actors are given or negotiate a privileged access. They are also associated with politicized processes of land formalization, which certain actors capture for their own benefit. Therefore, we need examining how the arrival of new investors fostered political struggles over land, capital and authority between and within governance levels. Unpacking these political interplays is key to understand what is going on, who is benefiting, who is losing and why it is unfolding this way. To put it bluntly, we need studying who the actors are and how they play this new farmland investment game to better explain its local impacts.

To do so, this book proposes an original analytical tool, CAS (explained below), which permits examining actors' interactions and analysing how they shape local outcomes associated with new farmland investments in Tanzania. In addition to CAS, which provides helpful and comprehensive lenses to analyse the local impacts of the land rush in developing countries, the book offers a novel, multi-dimensional perspective on the land rush by proposing an original analytical structure. Every chapter is focused on a specific level of governance,[1] a determined political arena in which investment dynamics and political relations are analysed. It permits the reader to have a detailed and simultaneous understanding not only of what is going on in specific political arenas but also of how all these political arenas are interconnected and interdependent. Such a structure is also more pragmatic and better connected to the experiences of international development actors and donors, who often deal with various actors at different levels of governance when they implement land projects or initiatives. The findings presented are based on extensive field research: a nine-month political ethnography[2] that I conducted between June 2016 and September 2017, mostly in two Tanzanian rural regions, Pwani and Kagera. Before outlining the chapters, the remainder of this introduction conceptualizes CAS.

CAS as a unified analytical tool

CAS is based on two assertions. First, local outcomes associated with farmland investments in Tanzania result from actors' interactions. I agree with White et al.'s proposal to consider how 'the micro-politics of negotiations of land control, access and exclusion [that] are played out at the local level' (2012, p. 633). Referring to 'Bernstein's Marxian haiku – Who owns what? Who does what? Who gets what? What do they do with it?' (Bernstein, 2010, p. 22), they suggest adding a fifth key question – what do they do to each other? – to capture the relational and political side associated with new farmland investments (White et al., 2012, p. 621). Indeed, local interactions are context-dependent, and not necessarily organized or constant across time and space: they are dynamic relational processes. They are contingent on investments' terms of inclusion and exclusion that are constantly being negotiated between a wide range of actors – local, national, transnational and international (Borras and Franco, 2013; Purdon, 2013; Castellanos-Navarrete and Jansen, 2015; Hall et al., 2015). Therefore, my first contention is that actors' interactions are determining the local outcomes associated with new farmland investments. A crucial question then is what shapes these interactions? This brings us to my second assertion. These interactions are shaped by the interplay between three main elements: contingencies (C), actors' agency (A) and structure (S). I use the acronym CAS to refer to these three elements. CASs produce the distribution of power among actors, which is structurally inegalitarian. In addition, CASs are context-dependent: the same local context may produce different CASs. Yet nothing is static within a given CAS. Dynamics may change relatively quickly, because of the interplay between its three constitutive elements. My claim is that analysing given local CASs, and how they develop through time and space, is key to grasping and differentiating actors' interactions that shape the local outcomes associated with new farmland investments.

To conceptualize CAS, and its constitutive elements, I purposefully adopt a perspective of analytical eclecticism. Sil and Katzenstein (2010, p. 412) define it as 'an intellectual stance a researcher can adopt when pursuing research that engages, but does not fit neatly within, established research traditions in a given discipline or field'. It involves two elements. First, my research process was foremost pragmatic, reflecting what Sil and Katzenstein call 'epistemological agnosticism'. It followed from a desire to engage with various research traditions to better explain and make sense of empirical data. Second, it was also holistic. I favoured a broad scope analytical process, seeking not only to engage but also to trace the complexity of the issues studied to understand how distinctive mechanisms interact, and how they explain actors' practices. I understand theories as specific lenses that are helpful in making sense of the world, but only if we acknowledge that they are by nature limitative – they circumscribe what we can see – and incomplete – they are never comprehensive enough. Therefore, using a set of sociological and political theoretical insights is helpful in exposing the complexity of the social world, contributing to an explanation of actors' social practices that have been observed in analytically circumscribed, spatialized and temporal situations.

Contingencies (C) are part of any social phenomena and may significantly impact structure (S) and actors' agency (A) in each situation. As a matter of fact, the whole 'land grabbing' phenomenon can be treated as a new contingency that had greatly impacted the country's political economy by offering access to new capital. As this book demonstrates, new farmland investments led to redefine actors' interactions at every governance level, in every political arena studied. Moreover, as I will show in Chapter 7, small contingencies, such as an increase in land prices, or the unexpected involvement of a member of Parliament (MP), are highly significant analytically even if they only provoked changes at the micro-level. Indeed, these changes offer new windows of opportunities that actors can and do seize to influence structural properties of given CASs. Consequently, I follow Sibeon's (White et al., 2012, p. 621) recommendation, and my analysis also systematically considers the importance of fortuity or social chance in any given social situation.

Drawing on the works of Ermakoff (2015, p. 69), I define contingencies through their 'essential causal indeterminacy' that is both exogenous and endogenous to the systems of interactions I analyse. This definition coalesces three considerations. First, contingencies pay attention to 'disruptions that are exogenous to the system of action being considered' (Ermakoff, 2015, p. 66), and as a result, they can be partly considered as happenstances. Yet, and second, this is reductive because indeterminacy is never properly exogenous. As noted by Ermakoff (2015, p. 66): 'it is also a property intrinsic to processes and events [...] in numerous instances, it is endogenous to the system of action it disrupts'. As a result, contingencies could always be better understood in studying the causality through an analysis of the endogenous. Therefore, using contingencies as an analytical category circumscribes the analysis. Yet, even if we can unpack the endogenous, the causality of contingencies can never be fully explained because contingencies also remained, by essence, and this is the third point, linked to the fundamental uncertainty of human agency.

'Against all odds, an individual can opt for a line of conduct eschewing the grips of conditioning factors' (Ermakoff, 2015, p. 76). In sum, contingencies then have both exogenous and endogenous properties, but are also essentially characterized by their causal indeterminacy. Within CAS, contingencies matter and are analytically important because they have a shaping effect on actors' interactions. The indeterminacy of social phenomena is also crucial in grasping why CASs vary in time and space.

To conceptualize structure (S) and agency (A), I favour analytical eclecticism and draw on historical institutionalism and on Giddens's theory of structuration. Historical institutionalism is helpful in conceptualizing how political institutions may structure local configurations of power and impact actors' agency. From a general standpoint, it is based upon the assumption that institutional frameworks are central to understand any political phenomenon because they both constrain actors' choices and offer opportunities by delimiting what is possible, and what is not (see discussion on New Institutionalism by Lowndes and Roberts, 2013, p. 7). More specifically, the historical institutionalist school defines institutions as 'formal and informal procedures, routines, norms, and conventions' (Hall and Taylor, 1996, p. 947) and focuses on the historical processes through which the institutional structure is constituted. One of its core assumptions is that institutions involve uneven distribution of power. Thus, it gives great importance to the study of the role played by institutions in enforcing asymmetrical power relations (Hall and Taylor, 1996, pp. 940–1). It highlights three mechanisms to explain how institutions work and constrain individuals' choices: rules (both formal and informal), practices and narratives. Rules specifically refer to laws and sanctions and are imposed through coercive mechanisms. Practices are associated with moral norms and obligations, enforcing and constituting at the same time the normative framework that gives cohesion and coherence to actors' actions. Finally, narratives are the reflection of a shared understanding (common beliefs and cognitive schemes) that is culturally constituted and commands compliance because of its taken-for-granted feature (Scott, 2001, p. 60; Lowndes and Roberts, 2013, p. 52). Yet historical institutionalism does not pay enough attention to the co-constitutive dynamic that is at play between structure/institutions and actors' agency. To address this shortcoming, CAS also integrates insights from Giddens's theory of structuration.

Giddens (2004) insists on the interplay between social practices and social systems. His compelling critique of functionalism and structuralism points out the need to better consider actors' agency in the production and reproduction of social structure. For Giddens, social systems have structural properties – symbolic, dominant and legitimizing – and express forms of domination and power. Giddens dismisses the very idea of objective external constraints that structure actors' actions. Instead, he argues for an interactionist view of social systems which are at the same time constraining and produced through social action with his idea of the duality of the structure. Thus, Giddens suggests that human agency and social structure are co-constitutive: through agents' social actions, the social structure is produced and reproduced. As Giddens puts it, 'Society only has form, and that form only has effects on people, insofar as structure is produced and reproduced in what people do' (Giddens and Pierson, 1998, p. 77).

Regarding agency, Giddens calls into question the concept of intentionality. Instead, he speaks of practical and discursive consciousness to emphasize the fact that much of quotidian activity is not purposefully motivated. For him, human agency refers to agents' capabilities in doing things, not necessarily to their intentions. Therefore, 'agency concerns events of which an individual is the perpetrator, in the sense that the individual could, at any phase in each sequence of conduct, have acted differently' (Giddens, 2004, p. 9). As Olivier de Sardan (2015, p. 41) puts it: '[Giddens's] agency designates the margin of appreciation and margin of manoeuvre available to all social actors, irrespective of the constraints under which they operate.' Giddens also emphasizes that agents' actions may have unintended consequences, which is a direct consequence of actors' unintentional and routinized actions. In his words: 'repetitive activities, located in one context of time and space, have regularized consequences, unintended by those who engage in those activities, in more or less "distant" time-space contexts' (Giddens, 2004, p. 14).

Although some structural properties are best understood as resulting from the duality of the social system – human agency and structure are co-constitutive – it is also significant and important to acknowledge that some of them are perceived by agents as objective external constraints. Socially constructed constraints may become objectified through time, and when it occurs, it hinders agents' capacity not only to change them, but also to question their very objective nature (Berger and Luckmann, 1968). For instance, even if they were, at one point in time-space, physical constraints may become almost immutable: their objectivation is so complete that actors generally conceive of them as given and inflexible. Furthermore, Giddens's definition of unintended consequences of human actions is somewhat limiting. They do not always result from non-intentional and routinized actions: they might also be unanticipated collateral effects of purposeful social practices. Indeed, actors may rationally and purposefully exert their agency but their capacity to fully control the consequences of their own agency is limited. As Diana Coole terms it: 'the operation of agentic capacities [...] will always exceed the agency exercised by rational subjects, even as these subjects acquire differential agentic capacities depending upon their intersubjective context' (Coole, 2005, qtd in Bennett, 2005, p. 453).

In sum, historical institutionalism and Giddens's theory of structuration are helpful starting points to conceptualize structure and agency. However, these theories' scope remains broad and general. Therefore, it is also crucial to specify some key institutional/structural features of the Tanzanian political settlement to better conceptualize CAS in SSA contexts. The state, for instance, is a key concept. Importantly, the state is not a unitary actor. Several scholars looking at the local impacts of land investments have pointed out the need to unpack political configurations to differentiate power struggles that are at play within the state and their impacts on political relationships (Peluso and Lund, 2011; Wolford et al., 2013; Pedersen, 2016; Buur, Nystrand and Pedersen, 2017). Similarly, an important scholarship on the nature of African states has highlighted the importance of shifting from state-centric perspectives to understand governance practices (Rasmussen and Strøh Varming, 2016). It has called attention to the fragmented and contentious authority of the state, highlighting the importance of delving into its multiple and competing authorities, each endowed with their own agenda, and interests. Indeed, considering the effects of this contentious and uneven state authority on actors' interactions is important. Consequently, I agree with Hagmann and Péclard and adopt Schlichte's definition of statehood as 'a field of power whose confines are decided upon with means of violence, and whose dynamics are marked by the ideal of a coherent, coercive, territorial organization as well as by the practices of social actors' (Schlichte, 2005, 106, qtd in Hagmann and Péclard, 2010, p. 546).

Moreover, the political settlement that prevails in Tanzania is shaped by relations of power, that I operationalize under two meta-types: clientelistic and infrastructural. My argument is that these two relations of power constitute inherent normative institutions of the Tanzanian political economy and should be systematically considered in relation to farmland investments.[3] To put it simply, new investments lead to commodification of land and new capital flows. Since clientelistic and infrastructural relations of power are preeminent, transversal and intertwined, these investments create incentives for state officials to use them to produce their political authority, which is key to access/create new accumulation opportunities. For instance, farmland investments have implications on clientelistic networks. In addition to the increase in revenues generated by the rent/sale of the land, they may foster the development of new infrastructures, or create local employment. Given the importance of clientelistic practices in many African states, and the blurring of limits between the private and public spheres, investors are likely to get involved in the web of informal clientelistic networks to increase return on investments. Of course, there is variance and power dynamics underlying actors' integration and opportunities within a given political economy, and its associated clientelistic networks. Simply, I term clientelistic relations of power to name these empirically observed relationships that resemble this relation of client to patron, with the client giving political or financial support to a patron in exchange for some personal, political or economic privilege or benefits (Lemarchand and Legg, 1972; Scott, 1972; Stokes, 2011).

In addition, the question of the state's capacity to implement its own rules and policies is relevant to the African context (Mann, 1984). Because of their specific mode of constitution, African states have had difficulty establishing control over their whole territory and population. Pastoral groups, for instance, have traditionally escaped state control because of their peripheral location and their nomadic livelihood (Hyden, 1980; Herbst, 2000). For the state, as Scott (1998) argues, increasing the legibility (e.g. through land titling, mapping, census, taxation) of these populations was crucial to asserting and strengthening its political control and legitimacy. Yet, as Scott also adds, many states have failed to achieve these objectives. Accordingly, Herbst (2000) has shown that expanding authority for rulers in Africa, from the precolonial to the postcolonial period, was heavily constrained by structural factors such as the geography, low population density, availability of land and their resources. Consequently, an important challenge for African states *still* is to build their authority over their whole territory. This pattern was already at play during the colonial period. Scholars such as Sara Berry (1993) showed the variation in colonial states' attempts at broadcasting their authority over their entire territory. As Berry (1993, p. 22) coined it, this was often 'hegemony on a shoestring', whereby 'the presence of the state in rural economies has been intrusive rather than hegemonic'.

Regarding farmland investments in Africa, scholars have put forward similar arguments showing that the state's involvement in land deals is not purely developmental or economically motivated: it is also often intertwined with the state officials' desire to strengthen their political and territorial authority over the periphery (Lavers, 2012; Lavers and Boamah, 2016; Hall and Kepe, 2017; Nalepa, Short Gianotti and Bauer, 2017). For example, Lavers and Boamah (2016) contend that agricultural investments might be used by the state to constitute its infrastructural power over an illegible society. As such, these deals contribute to the transformation of the state itself. As argued by Wolford et al. (2013, p. 194), 'land deals are nothing more or less than transformations in the ground on which states are formed'. In addition, further cogent evidence of the relevance of Scott's argument is found in mapping and land titling programmes that are currently implemented in many African states. Land policies are not necessarily reflective of or based upon pre-existing patterns of sovereignty. Rather, they are producing these patterns (Lund, 2011). Mapping and titling participate in the creative process of state formation: they are constitutive processes that produce state authority (Lund, 2013; Lund and Boone, 2013; Fogelman and Bassett, 2017). Therefore, land investments are intrinsically linked to land mapping and titling initiatives in Tanzania because authority over mapping and titling is key to establish state officials' power over land administration and investment negotiations. Infrastructural relations of power refer to this will of Tanzanian central authorities to assert their control over the countryside by rendering it more 'legible' and hence, administrable.

To conclude, it is with these theoretical insights that I conceptualize CAS. CAS is thus a unified analytical tool that helps us to better analyse, think and understand not only the short-term but also the longer-term effects of the land rush in developing countries. CAS is also a good analytical starting point for rethinking land development, investment and reform, and their implementation in Sub-Saharan Africa as it helps anticipating the challenges that might be encountered with implementation processes, and to mitigate them.

Outline of chapters

Chapter 2 situates the land rush issue at the global level. I argue that although the phenomenon triggered concerns and a global mobilization to protect developing countries' peasantry from land dispossession, it did not induce a deeper reconsideration of dominant development models. It is problematic because many assumptions underlying mainstream development thinking on farmland investments are misleading. To substantiate this point, I discuss how six of those fallacious assumptions do not hold up when we look at empirical evidence. For instance, I demonstrate that the claim that agricultural FDI would foster socio-economic development and favour poverty reduction by making productive use of 'idle or underused land' in SSA is inaccurate. I also discuss the role played by foreign investors, questioning their assumed competency and insisting on the importance of politicizing them as actors to understand how and why they play this farmland investment game. I conclude by reflecting on the impacts of those mainstream narratives on developing countries' peasantry. Not only this global S is shaping development agenda and initiatives, but it is also providing a rationale for national governments to justify dispossession and contentious political actions regarding land policies, formalization and investment as I have observed in Tanzania (see Chapter 4, national level; and Chapters 5 and 6, local level).

To introduce the next chapters and to situate the reader with regard to Tanzanian politics, **Chapter 3** first briefly examines Tanzania's historical trajectory, with a specific focus on land policies. This historical overview is crucial for understanding the land rights regime that prevails in Tanzania today. It also helps to elucidate the lasting paternalistic character of the relationship between the Tanzanian state and its citizens and explain why local resistance against the state in relation to land management is generally low. Second, it discusses the political context, devoting special attention to the two last elections (October 2015; October 2020). The 2015 elections were a key moment in Tanzania politics, exemplifying the intensity and the potency of factional struggles within the *Chama Cha Mapinduzi* (CCM).[4] Following an era of relative liberalization and an increase in political freedoms and rights throughout the country, the eruption of several corruption scandals illustrated that serious power struggles were at play within the CCM, rendering the balance between its political factions even more precarious than before. This political factionalism is a key variable in Tanzania to explain the centralization of land management and to capture clientelistic relationships between levels of governance. This chapter concludes by discussing recent political events, including the management of the Covid-19 crisis, the unexpected death of the elected President on 17 March 2021, and the beginnings of the presidency of his successor, Ms Samia Suluhu Hassan.

Chapter 4 analyses Tanzania's land discourses and policies in relation to this land rush. I show that there are important discrepancies between central government officials' pro-poor and pro-development official narrative, and their practices. Understanding these discrepancies requires us examining the politics inherent to the CAS structuring actors' interactions. More specifically, this chapter documents how and why central state officials seize opportunities opened up by contingencies – the renewed interest for farmland investments – to (re)shape the structure. I argue that state officials combine diverse normative rationalities – neoliberal development, capitalist exploitation, state-bureaucratic control, developmental paternalism, political clientelism – to justify institutional innovations that are foremost key to establish their control and power over land management. This creative process strengthens their political authority, which is strategic in capturing the economic opportunities that arise with those new farmland investments. It also justifies contentious political actions. I illustrate this argument with three recent examples. The first two examples, the discourse of the central state on productive investors and the review process of the National Land Policy, focus on the national level. The third example examines the implementation of the national programme for planning, surveying and land titling (PPSL) in two regions.

Yet, although Chapter 4 focuses on important political interactions which we need to capture to understand the local impacts associated with new farmland investments, such an understanding is not sufficient. The state is not a unitary actor, and its authority is contentious and limited. Therefore, as Migdal (1997, 2001) suggests, considering how national policies and discourses are transformed by actors throughout the implementation process is crucial to understanding the impact of their interactions, and governance practices on local communities.

Chapter 5 addresses Migdal's advice. In it, I unpack intermediaries and study how these actors negotiate their role with the central government, local populations and investors. This chapter shows that we should not overestimate the capacity of the central state. Given the fragmented and contentious nature of authority, state intermediaries also play an important role in negotiating norms and institutions to foster their own interests. More specifically, this chapter compares the involvement of two Tanzanian state agencies in land acquisition in Rufiji district, in the context of the central government's new strategy on productive investors that is discussed in Chapter 4. Chapter 5 shows that institutional change had direct consequences on the way local bureaucrats and a local state agency conduct their activities. Tanzanian central authorities lacked capacity, and as a result, there is a relation of dependency that exists between them and local bureaucrats. Because central state officials were dependent on local officials' knowledge, the latter found themselves in positions of power which they used to transform and alter central state policies during the implementation process. Moreover, by voluntarily misguiding central authorities, local bureaucrats were able to strengthen their authority and foster their interests with investors at the expense of the local population.

Chapter 6 adopts a local perspective and focuses on one specific and local investor, Kagera Sugar. To assess the impact of Kagera Sugar's arrival on the local agrarian political economy, I pay special attention to how 'the micro-politics of negotiations ..., access and exclusion are played out at the local level' (White et al., 2012, p. 633). This approach leads me to two main conclusions. First, Kagera Sugar's operational profitability reflects a commitment to cultivating clientelistic relations at the local and national level. Second, these clientelistic relations shape operational processes as well as local practices, fostering socio-economic differentiation in surrounding communities. This chapter highlights the role of clientelistic relations in shaping production activities and local practices. It shows that actors' political interactions between central and local levels are not always subversive or competitive (as discussed in Chapter 5), they can also be collaborative and interdependent. This interdependency is key here because it became the condition that underlies actors' position of authority in this local CAS. Furthermore, although this chapter illustrates how actors exert their agency to subvert or modify the structure to foster their interests, it also evidences that not all actors have the same capacity to influence it. There are structural inequalities in the distribution of power. As a result, it is primarily actors who hold enough power capital – political elites, investors and government officials – who can renegotiate the structure to further their political and material interests. Marginalized actors, because of their limited political capital, such as migrant workers, women and youths are often left out of this negotiation game, with very little leeway to influence the structure.

Chapter 7 further delves into those local dynamics and interactions, documenting at the micro-level how the expanding presence of investors in a Tanzanian village led to local land conflicts. It focuses on Village X which has been involved in two important land conflicts related to the arrival of new farmland investors. It seeks to explain a rather surprising finding: village leaders have defended their villagers' land rights in the first land conflict, but chose to partner with political elites and Tanzanian investors to foster their material interests at the expense of a sub-set of villagers in the other. Focusing on the very local set of actors' interactions structuring these conflicts in a specific Tanzanian village, I compare and explain why actors' interactions are different even in the same institutional context. My analysis emphasizes that actors' power holding is contingent in time and space, and insists on how formal and informal institutions are both constraining and enabling actors' agency. It also challenges the dominant narrative of Tanzania as a harmonious country in which ethnicity is not politically salient by showing that Tanzanian local actors have instrumentalized identity to produce political discrimination. In this specific region, historical legacies had created latent discrimination norms that once mobilized, created structural inequalities that affect certain actors' power.

Land and development governmentality: The international scene

This chapter focuses on the international governmentality (global CAS) associated with this global land rush, insisting on the structuring effect (S) of dominant discourses and narratives. I first discuss how the land rush was received on the global level. I argue that although land grabbing triggered concerns and a global mobilization to protect developing countries' peasantry from land dispossession, it did not induce a deeper reconsideration of dominant development models. It is problematic because many assumptions underlying mainstream development thinking on farmland investments are misleading. To substantiate this point, I discuss how six of those fallacious assumptions do not hold up when we look at empirical evidence. For instance, I demonstrate that the claim that agricultural FDI would foster socio-economic development and favour poverty reduction by making productive use of 'idle or underused land' in SSA is inaccurate. I also discuss the role played by foreign investors, questioning their assumed competency and insisting on the importance of politicizing them as actors to understand how and why they play this farmland investment game. I conclude by reflecting on the structuring impacts of those mainstream narratives in developing countries.

The land rush seen from above

It is on the international scene that the hype about this land rush first started. The 2011 World Bank publication *Rising Global Interest in Farmland: Can It Yield Sustainable and Equitable Benefits?* was a prime mover of the initial literature on land grabbing. It led to 'a veritable deluge [...] of op-eds, reports by non-governmental organizations (NGOs) and multilateral institutions, scholarly papers, books for specialist and non-specialist readers, and articles in leading social science and general science journals' (Edelman, 2013, p. 486). Most of those publications conveyed the same narrative.[1] According to the initial story, this land rush was resulting from the 2008 financial, energy and good supply global crises. The emphasis was put on the importance of financial speculation and of foreign investors in driving those new investment dynamics and on how such farmland investments are likely to negatively affect peasants from developing countries because of their tenure insecurity. In sum, the initial picture was rather dramatic and negative by describing these land deals as likely to disrupt the livelihoods of peasant/small-scale farmer communities, who were powerless in the face of such strong international pressures. The popularity of the use of 'land grabbing' speaks in itself of this negative connotation.

This global concern on the land rush also stimulated a discussion on how such investments can yield advantages for developing countries, and an awareness on the importance of assessing the implementation of such investments to achieve win-win solutions. International monitoring initiatives were put in place. For instance, international institutions created new governance mechanisms. Notably, the Food and Agriculture Organization (FAO) the World Bank (WB), the International Fund for Agricultural Development (IFAD) and the UN Conference on Trade and Development (UNCTAD), jointly elaborated the *Principles of Responsible Agricultural Investment* (*PRAI*). In 2012, the FAO further advanced international discussions on the issue by proposing its *Voluntary Guidelines on the Responsible Governance of Tenure of Land, Fisheries, and Forests* in the context of national food security, and more recently, in 2014, its *Principles for Responsible Investments in Agriculture and Food Systems* (*RAI*). The 2013 G8's Land Transparency Initiative was also a key international policy initiative. Moreover, two main international databases on land deals were developed: GRAIN's and the Land Matrix. GRAIN is a civil society organization, while the Land Matrix is the result of an initiative of the International Land Coalition, which brings together research and funding organizations. Their aim was similar: to provide a central point of reference that presents primary information on this land rush. Although it is true that these databases suceeded in providing a rough picture of what was going on globally, important methodological issues limited the validity of their data

(i.e. registered land deals that never materialized, duplication of data, false information on certain deals, etc.)

Nevertheless, the elaboration and adoption of those global monitoring mechanisms show that global actors came together to better monitor this land rush and its local impacts. However, and importantly, this global concern did not lead to fundamentally question the belief that farmland investments are key to foster agricultural modernization and development in developing countries. This neoliberal belief is based on the expectation that investors, by undertaking commercial agricultural ventures in developing countries, will favour productivity increase and stimulate local socio-economic development through technological transfers and employment creation. This vision is further strengthened by this persisting idea that SSA has plenty of 'idle' or 'unproductively used land' that awaits development opportunities. In parallel to this neoliberal discourse, new farmland investments have also been increasingly legitimized on the international scene through an eco-modernization discourse. Because of green farmland investments' potential for a triple win, 'climate change mitigation, poverty reduction and environmental protection', they have gained momentum in donors' and investors' circles (Bergius, Benjaminsen and Widgren, 2017, p. 827; Kish and Fairbairn, 2018). Distancing themselves from capitalist predatory practices associated with 'land grabbing', those investors brand themselves for their environmentally and socially responsible land investments in developing countries (Olwig et al., 2015; Bergius, Benjaminsen and Widgren, 2017; Kansanga and Luginaah, 2019; Jimenez-Soto, 2021). Yet such a green development/investment agenda continues framing SSA as the source of abundant and untapped resources, 'a site where global scarcities may be resolved' (Scoones et al., 2019, p. 231). Nor does it question this idea that SSA needs foreign investors to modernize agricultural practices and get out of poverty.

Additionally, both those narratives frame the problem resulting from this global land rush in terms of peasants' tenure insecurity. It is because peasants' rights are not formalized that they are vulnerable to land grabbing and/or do not benefit (enough) from those investments. The underlying idea is that this land rush could become a golden opportunity for developing countries if we can formalize the poors' land rights and make sure that farmland investments are successfully monitored to bring out the expected outcomes in terms of socio-economic development and environmental protection. Formalization of land rights then became the international advocacy solution to this land rush. However, as many scholars have pointed out, such an insistence on the formalization of land rights as the panacea to land insecurity of the poor is problematic. It depoliticizes the land question and reduces it to a technical fix. On the practical level, it assumes due diligence and does not consider the strong elite bias that exists in land administration, and in the conception and implementation of any land formalization programme. Key political questions are left unaddressed. For instance, is formalization really increasing peasants' tenure security? How are these programmes considering pre-existing structural inequalities which can influence access to land formalization programmes? What happens when elites and government officials make existing rights invisible? Who is really benefiting from land formalization? On a more meta-level, it does not question the relevance of land privatization and formalization in non-Western contexts. It seems then legitimate to ask whose tenure security is really strengthened.

Continuing along this critical line of reflection, the remainder of this chapter demonstrates that these global narratives on agricultural development, land formalization, land commodification, socio-economic development, productivity and investment are fallacious and inaccurate when we look at available current evidence. Indeed, they are based on many unquestioned and unproven assumptions. It is an important issue because those assumptions still frame mainstream development thinking on land issues and agricultural development, which has deleterious effects on developing countries' peasantry. To substantiate my point, I hereafter analyse six of those misleading assumptions.

Misleading assumptions on farmland investments, development and investors

First, to use Makki's (2014) expression, the terra nullius zones, the beliefs that SSA is a site of abundant resources and has plenty of idle, marginal or underused land, are part of a persistent myth. Everywhere in SSA, land scarcity is a problem. In addition, most investors are not acquiring marginal or idle land in developing countries: they are primarily targeting prime agricultural farmland, already used by smallholders and located near water sources and infrastructure, thereby finding themselves in direct competition with local populations over water and land access and control (Borras, 2011; Boche and Anseeuw, 2017; Nalepa, Short Gianotti and Bauer, 2017; Hindeya, 2018; Tufa, Amsalu and Zoomers, 2018; Arnall, 2019; Glover and Jones, 2019; Persson, 2019).

Second, employment creation seems to be usually a short-term effect with limited evidence of lasting economic impacts. Newly created jobs are usually seasonal, low-qualified and temporary (Schoneveld, German and Nutakor, 2010; Murray Li, 2011; Alhassan, Shaibu and Kuwornu, 2018; Bluwstein et al., 2018; Ayelazuno, 2019). Moreover, as Chapter 6 demonstrates, even if some farmland investments bring positive socio-economic outcomes, those benefits are often unevenly distributed at the local level. Farmland investments thus do not necessarily benefit everyone and may worsen the situation of the most vulnerable populations by making them landless without much alternative to make a living.

Third, despite the pretentions associated with what is framed as environmentally and socially responsible farmland investments in developing countries, evidence points out that there is no significant difference in the local impacts of such investments when compared with more mainstream investments (Kish and Fairbairn, 2018). They tend to induce similar local outcomes, also leading to land dispossession and exclusion (Olwig et al., 2015; Bergius, Benjaminsen and Widgren, 2017; Engström, 2018; Kansanga and Luginaah, 2019; Jimenez-Soto, 2021). Reviewing the local impacts of three Scandinavian 'green' large-scale agricultural investments, Bergius et al. (2017, p. 842) remark: 'The ostensibly "benevolent" Scandinavian states, development agencies and businesses [...] are no different from other powerful actors in the way their land investment practices tend to be blind to the dispossession and social injustice following in their wake'. Perhaps then, the key difference only lies in how investors legitimized their projects.

Fourth, persistent beliefs such as foreign investors are more productive than local farmers and African agriculture is characterized by its 'intrinsic lower productivity', its backward technology, and smallholders' 'slowness' to adopt modern farming do not hold when faced with the facts (Christiaensen, 2017, p. 9; Sheahan and Barrett, 2017; Snyder et al., 2020). For instance, scholars have showed that peasants' decision on using inputs does not result from their backwardness and/or their resistance and ignorance towards modern farming. Instead, underemployment (Christiaensen, 2017, p. 7; Davis, Di Giuseppe and Zezza, 2017), national policies (Sheahan and Barrett, 2017), unreliable markets, and the size of land parcels (Aha and Ayitey, 2017; Snyder et al., 2020) have been identified as causal factors in explaining their lower use of agricultural inputs. Also, many studies have showed that large- and small-scale producers have comparable levels of productivity, even though the formers' use of input is greater (Hules and Singh, 2017; Deininger and Xia, 2018). Moreover, even if small-scale farmers have average lower yield than their commercial counterparts, their potential to improve productivity by hectare is superior because they have a better adaptation capacity and can capitalize on the added value of their land (Karsenty, 2018). Importantly, the environmental costs induced by commercial farming methods are usually not qualified or quantified as financial externalities in these comparisons over productivity (Fig, 2011; Persson, 2019).

Fifth, foreign investors are not necessarily competent and efficient. In fact, numerous investors are ill-equipped and/or incompetent to undertake such ambitious farmland investments projects, in SSA and elsewhere. Many investors have unrealistic business expectations and business plans (Goetz, 2015; Ahmed, Campion and Gasparatos, 2017) and failed to undertake the relevant studies and assessments before investing in their proposed projects (Gerlach and Liu, 2010; Nwibo and Okorie, 2013; Anseeuw and Boche, 2015; Di Matteo and Schoneveld, 2016; Ahmed, Campion and Gasparatos, 2019). Investors' lack of environmental knowledge (suitability of soils, flooding patterns, seeds compatibility, etc.) also plays a role in explaining their incapacity to make production economically viable (Gill, 2016; Ahmed, Campion and Gasparatos, 2019; Antwi-Bediako et al., 2019). In his analysis of the Karuturi project in Ethiopia, Gill (2016) specifically identified the company's epistemological assumptions and lack of local knowledge as the main cause of the project failure. Historical and current initiatives to foster a commercial agricultural model in Gambella region led to localized deforestation. This created abnormal flood patterns and reduced the capacity of the land to absorb water. Ultimately, it is those floods, and Karuturi's inability to compose with them that made the investment fail. In their analysis of the drivers of the collapse of jatropha projects in Ghana, Ahmed et al. (2019, p. 332) indicate that lack of basic agronomic knowledge about jatropha led to low productivity that reduced these projects' economic viability. In addition, many investors underestimate the settling and transaction costs associated with such ambitious business propositions. In Africa, these costs are particularly high: infrastructures are underdeveloped, there is a lack of local markets to buy inputs and commercialize production and bringing land to production might reveal much more expensive than expected (Anseeuw and Boche, 2015; Visser, 2015). The governance context and institutional deficiencies may render projects more complicated and unpredictable than initially envisioned. Indeed, securing land rights, permits and authorizations and negotiating with local communities may reveal lengthy and challenging, creating unanticipated expenses and delays (on the role of delays, see Engström, 2018). For instance, in Mozambique, although the company claimed it 'followed the process to secure the land without impacting negatively the communities', it was allocated a densely populated area and left without government's help or guidance into how to displace and compensate affected farmers (Arnall, 2019, p. 866). As a result of all those factors, many investors found themselves lacking the financial resources to develop or operationalize such massive land investments, leading many projects into a 'cash trap'[2] (Spoor, 2012; Bräutigam and Zhang, 2013; Nwibo and Okorie, 2013; Anseeuw and Boche, 2015; Schönweger and Messerli, 2015; Di Matteo and Schoneveld, 2016; Kuns and Visser, 2016).

Sixth, investors are political actors, and their motivations are messier and blurrier that assumed by such mainstream narratives. Clearly, farmland investors face important political and infrastructural challenges[3] that reduce their productivity potential in the short run and appear to offset the advantages of acquiring cheap land in developing countries. As McCarthy, Vel and Afiff (2012, p. 535) similarly observe, it raises the question of why the land is acquired if it is unlikely that it could be put to production. The scholarship lists many other motivations behind those land acquisitions: money laundering, tax evasion (Spoor, 2012; GRAIN, 2016; McSweeney et al., 2017), subsidies, speculation, asset stripping (McCarthy, Vel and Afiff, 2012; Spoor, 2012; Visser, Mamonova and Spoor, 2012) or even what Visser et al. (2012) name 'tacit political agreements' in reference to the hidden arrangement in Russia between investors and the Kremlin.[4] As Keene et al. put it (2015, p. 132): 'The sources and reasoning behind land deals are often contingent and messy and lands are identified (and constructed) as "grabbable" for a wide variety of reasons'. Indeed, motivations behind those large-scale farmland acquisitions are contingent, might be conflicting, change in time and space and are often illegible (Keene et al., 2015, p. 141). To further substantiate this point on investors' hidden motivations, the next sections detail two investment cases that I have investigated in Tanzania.

Investors' hidden motivations: Example 1

A first example is this foreign company owned by two Indian brothers who acquired, in 2013, derivative land rights on 1,301 hectares to grow maize in Rufiji district (hereafter called Investor X). The land acquisition process was top-down, lacked transparency and involved top officials from the President's office and the Ministry for lands. In addition, consultation and compensation of local affected communities were unsatisfactory as many villagers were left uninformed of the deal until it was concluded. Even if it is true that the company acquired old farming machinery and established a local office in an adjacent village, it was never operational. In the village where the company acquired land: I found no physical evidence of the company presence.

Although the underlying motivations of Investor X are difficult to pinpoint with certainty, my findings strongly indicate that agricultural production was not its primary motive. A first possibility was that Investor X probably acquired this land to capture parts of the local agricultural trade. The adjacent village where it established its office is located about 200 kilometres from Dar es Salaam, the main and biggest commercial city of Tanzania. Most local producers sell their harvests to brokers, who then resell them in the city. It is a lucrative business because those brokers enjoy huge profit margin by exploiting rural farmers who lack local markets to sell their production. However, trader permits are expensive and difficult to obtain in Tanzania. Owning rights on agricultural land provides a solution to overcome the difficulty of entering the trading business: it allows investors to conduct trading activities without the trading permit. Based on the interviews I conducted, the owners have engaged in some trading activities, and this might be one plausible explanation of why Investor X acquired this parcel of land.

A second possibility is that acquiring land allows the company to access substantial funding. In 2014, the company secured an important mortgage with the Development Bank of Tanzania (TIB), using its derivative rights on the land as a collateral for an agricultural loan. Although research on the links between farmland acquisitions, subsidies and bank loans is still sparse, other scholars have documented similar dynamics (McCarthy, Vel and Afiff, 2012; see also the chapter on Ethiopia in Cochrane and Andrews, 2021, p. 230). The company secured funding that was worth 262 times its annual land renting payment. As this number shows, in Tanzania, there is a huge gap between the government and commercial banks' valuation of farmland assets. Concretely, it means that investors, by acquiring rights on agricultural land, may access substantial funding from commercial banks with a minimal amount of capital. This is what this company did. However, in 2016, Investor X defaulted on its loan repayments to the TIB and was placed under receivership. Legally then, the TIB became the owner of Investor X's assets and land rights, which were then duly evaluated. According to the lawyer in charge of this case, it is during this evaluation process that they realized that Investor X has reallocated its agricultural funding to other projects. The company's few agricultural assets were mostly broken and worthless, meaning that agricultural funding has been diverted. Since the owners are Indian, TIB's legal procedures against them were complexified because the bank has no legal recourse or authority in India. The fact that one of the owners died in 2014 and the other one has left the country further complicated TIB's legal procedures, which were still ongoing in 2017. In sum, it seems very unlikely that the TIB will recover its financial loss regarding the loan attributed to the company. Investor X's case is far from being exceptional in Tanzania. In the words of one lawyer specialized in the management of similar receivership issues: 'It is very common for businesses to do that in Tanzania. Investors in this country know the loopholes in the law and use them' (interview lawyer CRB, 12.2016).

Investors' hidden motivations: Example 2

A second example is provided with the case of a South African company. The owner is South African and a resident of Kenya (hereafter called Investor Z). He has other business ventures in East Africa, namely in South Sudan and in Kenya. After a lengthy process that started back in 2008, he acquired in 2015 the derivative land title for 5,506.8 hectares in Rufiji district to grow rice. More specifically, this land is located at the border of the Selous Game Reserve (Selous) – a 54,600 square kilometres protected area (in 2019, an area of over 30,000 square kilometres of the Selous was turned into the new Nyerere National Park). It is quite isolated as transportation is disrupted during the rainy season due to flooding. The Selous is one of the few game reserves in Tanzania that allows for game hunting, a luxury and lucrative touristy activity that is heavily monitored and taxed by government authorities. Four villages have been affected by this land acquisition. The investor has promised them to grow rice, put in place an irrigation scheme and provide employment for locals. In addition, he committed to disburse every year, to each four villages, a contribution in-cash to facilitate development. According to the investor's story, although he has already invested US$ 1 million, his failure to develop commercially the land for his agricultural project resulted from different factors: a strenuous and lengthy farmland negotiation/acquisition process; the difficulty to secure funding; massive investment required to make this land productive; and an unclear commercial value of the land (interview with Investor Z, 08.2017). Yet, when I visited Investor Z's farm in December 2016, there was no visible trace of the investor's claimed initial investment. Despite the Tanzanian Investment Center (TIC)[5] and district officials' repeated statements that the investor has started to clear the road leading to his land since 2015, as of 2017, the road in question revealed being nothing much that a sandy path, obviously unsuitable to commercial transportation.[6] In short, there was no physical indicator to substantiate the investor's claim that he intended to start production in a near future.

Based on my field observations, data collected and interviews, it became clear to me that Investor Z did not acquire this land for rice production. However, as with Investor X, it is impossible to identify with certainty the exact motivations behind this land acquisition. Two explanations seem plausible. The first one is speculation. Speculation on land has been depicted as a key driver of land acquisitions (Collier and Venables, 2012; Dell'Angelo et al., 2017). Since the 2008 crises, one of the reasons farmlands have gained momentum amongst financial investors is because they assumed that its appreciation will lead to appreciable financial returns (Fairbairn, 2014, p. 10). Yet turning agricultural land into a financial asset is a tricky business. Although land has a dual nature – the potential to be both a productive and a financial asset – its potential to become a financial asset remains tricky because land is also characterized by its immobility and the difficulty to be transformed into a liquidity (Knuth, 2015, p. 168; Magnan, 2015; see also Visser, 2015). Reaping the benefits of land appreciation in a relatively short-term horizon is therefore less straightforward than expected and at odds with the logic of what Kaarhus (2018) calls 'the impatience of capital'. It led several investors to abandon projects when they realized their anticipated benefits are not materializing rapidly enough. Land commodification and financialization are thus 'uneven process[es] that can also lead to failed investments, revealing the potential contradictions between the logics and temporalities of finance and agriculture' (Sippel, Larder and Lawrence, 2017, p. 252). This hypothesis is supported by the investor's own contradictory statements during our meeting in August 2017. Although he kept telling me that he was committed to develop his land into a viable and commercial agricultural venture, he also trusted me with the fact that he was not able to access sufficient funding to do so, and that he wanted to get rid of this farmland and its associated problems. At the end of our interview, he told me that he was now planning to meet with an 'Indonesian conglomerate looking to acquire 100,000 ha' and that he was 'hoping to sell them the idea that they can use his land for seeds' (interview with Investor Z, 08.2017).

A second explanation that was suggested by several informants, including district officials and local villagers, is that Investor Z acquired this land for private hunting. The land is located just outside of the Selous and appears much more suitable for wildlife hunting than for agricultural production. Moreover, before being transferred to Investor Z, this land was used by local population mostly for illegal poaching activities. Significantly, the land acquired is in the northern part of the four affected villages, as near as possible to the Selous boundaries. The fact that the investor is a hunter also give credence to this claim. He told me that he used to hunt near the Ngorongoro Crater, Arusha region, but also that he undertook a hunting trip on the south side of his land (interview with Investor Z, 08.2017). In sum, as these two examples show, assuming that investors' first interest is to develop agricultural production when acquiring farmland is misleading. Their motivations and interest are often blurry and deserve further in-depth empirical investigation.

To conclude, on the international scene, this land rush raised serious concerns and led to the adoption of global monitoring and governance mechanisms that aim at protecting the land rights of developing countries' peasants. Yet mainstream narratives and their underlying assumptions on investment and agricultural development were not questioned. Further problematic is the fact that many of those assumptions are fallacious. As this book will demonstrate, by producing and reproducing those narratives on investment, agricultural and socio-economic development, land formalization and commodification, many international actors depoliticize land issues and agricultural development initiatives. This has lasting and dramatic consequences for the peasantry of developing countries. On the one hand, the assumption on their backwardness and inability to develop productively their assets justifies massive land transfers to investors, foreign or local. In addition, such global narratives effectively exclude peasants from both international and national agricultural development agendas. Even in cases where local communities are involved in the development agenda, such as in Liberia (Roesch, 2021) where management is participatory, the effects of such global discourses are pervasive. For instance, communities may internalize the international rhetoric associated with resource conservation, even if it outlaws their traditional local uses and effectively deter them from using forest resources. As Roesch (2021, p. 154) remarks: 'The strong development discourse accompanying the formalization of the community forest contributed to silencing and criminalizing those negatively affected.' It may also lead to development aberrations as Attah (2021) reports with the case of Shonga Farms in Nigeria. Rather than supporting its own farmers, the Nigerian government invested massively to support a foreign investor.

> The government invested over N400 million (US$ 2.6 million) on roads, housing and electricity; each farmer received a bungalow of up to 2500

square feet, complete with a generator, storage sheds, and fencing. N870 million (US$ 5.8 million) was spent on irrigation by the federal government while N1 billion (US$ 6.6 million) was provided for electrification.

(Attah, 2021, p. 125)

The project finally collapsed. One might wonder what would have happened if such governmental support has been given to Nigerian farmers.

On the other hand, as the Tanzanian case exemplifies, such global narratives indirectly legitimize and consolidate state's infrastructural violence, exclusion and dispossession processes against peasants. State officials and elites use of their political powers to interfere in land formalization and acquisition processes to secure new rents and secure their participation to new sites of accumulation created by this land rush. Moreover, as a result, state officials and elites tend to disregard investors' lack of productivity or unfulfilled local development promises. The immediate result is land dispossession with few socio-economic benefits for affected communities. Given the fact that statutory and customary regimes are still overlapping in many SSA countries and that customary rights tend to be less respected, dispossessed peasants are often left with very few options to defend their land rights.

3

In brief, historical land management in Tanzania and factional struggles within the CCM

To introduce the next chapters, and to situate the reader with regard to Tanzanian politics, this chapter first briefly introduces Tanzania's historical trajectory, with a specific focus on land policies. This historical overview is crucial for understanding the land rights regime that prevails in Tanzania today. It helps to elucidate the lasting paternalistic character of the relationship between the Tanzanian state and its citizens and explain why local resistance against the state in relation to land management is generally low. Second, it discusses the political context, devoting special attention to the two last elections (October 2015; October 2020). The 2015 elections were a key moment in Tanzania politics, exemplifying the intensity and the potency of factional struggles within the CCM. Following an era of relative liberalization and an increase in political freedoms and rights throughout the country, the eruption of several corruption scandals illustrated that serious power struggles were at play within the CCM, rendering the balance between its political factions even more precarious than before. This political factionalism is a key variable in Tanzania to explain the centralization of land management, and to capture clientelistic relationships between levels of governance. This chapter concludes by discussing recent political events, including the Covid-19 crisis, the unexpected death of the elected President on 17 March 2021, and the beginnings of the presidency of his successor, Ms Samia Suluhu Hassan.

The legacies of historical land management

Access to land was and remains to this day a crucial and salient political question in Tanzania, as most Tanzanians live in rural areas and practice subsistence agriculture. The Tanzanian territory is approximately 945,087 square kilometres, with an estimated arable land area of 888,200 square kilometres. Despite the large amount of land, low rainfall and poor soil fertility explain low population density and the prevalence of shifting cultivation and pastoralism (World Bank, 2010). Already during the colonial era, land was a political question in Tanganyika. The Land Ordinance of 1923, established by the British colonial administration, was instrumental in centralizing Tanzania's land management. Following its enactment, the colonial governor became solely responsible for land allocation (Shivji, 1992, 2006). Later, British authorities, following the recommendation of the African Royal Commission 1953–1955, sought to render effective another policy titled The Individualization, Titling and Registration (ITR) which aimed at transforming customary land management to allow private ownership of land in Tanzania. Julius Nyerere, the charismatic leader of the Tanganyika African National Union (TANU), vigorously opposed this colonial land commercialization initiative. It became part of the political grievances fuelling Tanzania's fight for Independence. In his 1958 pamphlet, *Mali ya Taifa*, Nyerere already presented his vision of what should be the land management precepts of Tanzania:

> In a country such as Tanzania, where, generally speaking, the Africans are poor and the foreigners are rich, it is quite possible that, within eighty or a hundred years, if the poor African were allowed to sell his land, all the land in Tanganyika would belong to wealthy immigrants, and the local people would be tenants. But even if there were no rich foreigners in this country, there would emerge rich and clever Tanganyikans. If we allow land to be sold like a robe, within a short period there would only be a few Africans possessing land in Tanganyika and all the others would be tenants. (Julius Nyerere, 1966, qtd in Haki Ardhi) (Land Rights Research and Resources Institute (LRRRI), 2010)

Under Julius Nyerere's leadership, in 1961, Tanganyika won its independence from Great Britain. Tanzania itself was created in 1964 with the union of Zanzibar and Tanganyika. Inspired by the Soviet experience, Nyerere established in the newly formed Tanzania a socialist-inspired system of governance, based on the full powers of a single party. Nyerere's approach was paternalistic: only enlightened leaders were thought to have the ability to guide their people in development. This choice was further justified by the lingering distrust of European institutions, largely due to the colonial era, and the fear that political dissent might hurt the country's economic development (Ekeh, 1975; Constant Martin, 1988).

After Independence, following *Azimio la Arusha* – the Arusha Declaration, the new Tanzanian state implemented two new land policies: The 1967 Land Acquisition Act No. 47 which was followed by the well-known the 1975 Ujamaa Village Act No. 21. The *ujamaa* policy was envisioned as an experiment of socialism and self-reliance. It was first presented by Nyerere as a means to improve the living conditions of the poorest, and to involve and empower the peasantry in its own development. It led to a massive country-wide villagization project that entailed the relocation of Tanzanian rural populations into government-created villages that were deemed more suitable for development, in terms of planning, infrastructure and social services. Politically, the policy also aimed to increase the state's power over Tanzanian rural regions (Iliffe, 1979; Hyden, 1980; Lorgen, 2000; Schneider, 2004; Fouéré, 2011). Finally, this policy made the Tanzanian state (with the President's prerogative) the sole owner of all Tanzanian land. Yet, despite Nyerere's official discourse and vision, villagization was a national project violently imposed on Tanzania's rural population. As noted by Young (1988), this policy, its ideational background and the way it was implemented echoed the colonial practices so virulently decried by Nyerere. Schneider (2004, p. 347) also highlights this paradox between Nyerere's discourse and practices, when he explains that: 'on the question of Nyerere's role in *ujamaa*/villagization, [...] the President was central in driving rural development into coercive directions, which, at other times, he so forcefully spoke out against'. Indeed, speaking of a 'forced Tanzanian villagization' would be more accurate, as the *ujamaa* policy led to the forceful displacement of a large part of the Tanzanian population in the 1970s (Ingle, 1970). Of course, despite the inherent contradictions of the policy, not everything has been negative, and scholars have called for more nuanced accounts on the impacts of the *ujamaa* policy on Tanzanians. Mbilinyi (2016), for instance, contends that forced villagization was not true in all locations, and that in some cases, it led to the empowerment of Tanzanian women.

In the end though, the *ujamaa* policy proved a failure and had lasting effects on spatial relations all over Tanzania. Estimates are that it led to the displacement of no less than 66.6 per cent of the population (Young, 1997, pp. 113–44). In addition, villagization had pernicious effects on the land tenure system. As noted by Swantz (1996), 'In Tanzania [...] many people were settled on land belonging to other villagers and were uncertain of future claims to the land. The commodification of village land in Tanzania was one of the many unintended consequences of villagization resulting from the disruption of the land tenure system' (Swantz, 1996, 147, qtd in Lorgen, 2000, p. 185).

Bankruptcy and liberalization

From the beginning of the 1980s, the Tanzanian socialist welfare state imagined by Nyerere proved inviable. An important financial crisis, combined with general state bankruptcy, forced Nyerere to ask for international support. In fact, the Tanzanian state could no longer financially support its development projects and the needs of its population. International financial institutions, heavily influenced by the prevailing neoliberal ideology at the time, conditioned aid and loans on the implementation of structural adjustment plans. Nyerere initially rejected their conditions. Refusing to implement the requested reforms himself, he retired in 1985. The succeeding President, Ali Hassan Mwinyi, accepted the structural adjustment plan. He liberalized the economy (free trade and privatization of state enterprises), introduced a multi-party political system, reduced the size of the state and substantially limited government expenditures in public services. In addition to demanding the liberalization of the economy and the democratization of governance, the International Monetary Fund (IMF) and the World Bank also mandated the abolition of subsidies to agriculture[1] that were perceived as economically inefficient. The withdrawal of the state from agriculture put Tanzanian farmers into an even more precarious situation: the liberalization period led to a significant decline in the country's agricultural productivity and production (Skarstein, 2005, pp. 340–4). These neoliberal reforms did not have the desired impacts (Maruba, 2008, pp. 62–4; Lofchie, 2014). Politically, the CCM remained the unchallenged ruling party in Tanzania – the CCM was created in 1977, following the union of TANU, with the Afro-Shirazi Party (ASP – the ruling party in Zanzibar). Economically, structural adjustment led to the growing political use of these international funds to ensure the stability of the ruling Tanzanian elite, and at the same time, a significant withdrawal of the state in social and development policies (van de Walle, 2001, p. 96). The state's lack of accountability to its donors and citizens, and the fact that not fulfilling the conditions imposed did not diminish the international aid granted partly explain this outcome.

As the financial crisis worsened, civil servants took advantage of their governmental positions to engage in rent-seeking through permits, quotas, taxes and subsidies and put in place mechanisms that allowed them to increase their personal income. For instance, the privatization of state-owned companies and national estates benefited many influential Tanzanians (Lofchie, 2014, pp. 23–4). Corruption was rampant and still is an important issue. Transparency International, in its 2020 Corruption Perception Index, gave Tanzania a score of 38 in terms of transparency, on a scale of 0 (highly corrupt) to 100 (very clean). The country is ranked 94 out of 180 countries (Transparency International 2020). This propensity for corruption is also evidenced in popular language. Indeed, the initials of the party, the CCM (*Chama Cha Mapinduzi*), are commonly reappropriated to reformulate the name of the party by the population. For instance, Tanzanians prefer to talk about *Chukua Chako Mapema* (take yours as fast as you can) or *Chama Cha Majangili* (the party of crooks) (Tripp, 1997, p. 180). Similarly, to denounce the fact that several officials use their position in the government and their access to public resources to enrich themselves personally, Tanzanians have renamed the National Economic Survival Program (NESP) as the Personal Economic Survival Program.

In addition, the gradual withdrawal of the Tanzanian state from social affairs led to the deterioration of public services. For example, in 1969, 90 per cent of the urban population had access to drinking water. This number drastically decreased from the 1980s to only 56 per cent in 1993. Also, the purchasing power of the civil service fell by 94 per cent in real dollars between 1969 and 1985 (Tripp, 1997). In addition, primary school attendance, which was 98 per cent in 1980 fell at 70 per cent in 1997 (Pinkney, 2001). As Tripp (1997, p. 130) describes it: 'Schools in Buguruni and Manzese [a neighborhood of Dar es Salaam] had virtually no textbooks, notebooks, charts, or even desks or chairs. Nor did they have equipment with which to teach vocational skills'. This socialist state's failure and the turn towards liberalization had dramatic effects not only on the economy, but also on the relationship between the state and the citizens. Since the Nyerere era, the postcolonial state was built primarily as a source of profit distribution to ensure social equality and a national project of socio-economic development. By failing at that very function in the 1980s and the 1990s, the state lost its credibility, and this led to citizens' progressive disengagement from the state entity (Ayoade, 1988; Tripp, 1997).

Land rights remained at the heart of the newly liberalized government's concerns. However, new land laws departed from Nyerere's socialist vision. Rather, heavily influenced by neoliberal precepts, they promoted private and individual land rights to foster smallholders' productivity, reduce poverty and ensure economic growth (Skarstein, 2005). More specifically, this vision led to two new Land Acts: The Land Act No. 4 and the Village Land Act No. 5. They were ratified in 1999, and became effective in 2001. Unlike the previous British law, these new Land Acts established the legal equivalence of granted and customary land rights (Sulle and Nelson, 2009, p. 37). Another important innovation of this new legislative land framework was that foreigners were now able to acquire derivative Tanzanian land rights. Although these laws still constitute to this day the legal framework governing land rights and ownership in Tanzania, a process of revising the National Land Policy is currently underway (a detailed discussion on the land policies is presented in Chapter 4).

In sum, the Tanzanian state model that emerged during this liberalization period was characterized by its hybridity, its blurred boundaries between public and private spheres and its lack of capacity. Borrowing Mbembe's expression (2010), Tanzania's governance became and still is characterized by its political diffraction. The term 'diffraction' is borrowed from physics, literally meaning an optical phenomenon of deviation. Adapting it, Mbembe (2010, p. 24) speaks of the great social diffraction: 'This diffraction of society led to the informalization of social and economic relations, unprecedented fragmentation of the field of rules and norms, and a process of deinstitutionalization that has not spared the state itself'.

Table 1 Key historical events and land policies

Date	Historical moments	Legal land framework	Highlights
1923		Land Ordinance Act	Made the colonial governor the sole responsible for land allocation
1953–5		The Individualization, Titling and Registration (ITR) policy	Aimed at transforming customary land management to allow private ownership of land (was heavily contested)
1954	Creation of the TANU (Tanganyika African National Union)		
1961	Independence of Tanganyika under Julius Nyerere		
1963	Tanzania is created (union of Zanzibar and Tanganyika)		
1967		Land Acquisition Act No. 47	Repeals and replaces the 1923 Land Acquisition Ordinance
			Provides for compulsory acquisition of lands for public purposes (including housing scheme)
1975		Ujamaa Village Act No. 21 (Arusha Declaration)	Allows for the relocation of Tanzanian rural populations into government-created villages. Made the Tanzanian state (with the President's prerogative) the sole owner of all Tanzanian land
1977	Creation of the CCM with the union of TANU and the Afro-Shirazi Party (ASP—the ruling party in Zanzibar)		

Date	Historical moments	Legal land framework	Highlights
1985	Resignation of Julius Nyerere		
1985	The new President Ali Hassan Mwinyi accepts the structural adjustment plan proposed by the FMI and the World Bank		
1995		National Land Policy	Lays the general principles of land management
1995–2005	Tanzania's President is Benjamin Mkapa (replacing Mwinyi)		
1999		Land Act No. 4 Village Land Act No. 5	Classifies land in three categories: general, reserved and village
			Maintains the President's prerogative on land
			Established the legal equivalence of granted and customary land rights
			Allows foreigners to acquire derivative Tanzanian land rights
2005–15	Tanzania's President is Jakaya Kikwete (replacing Mkapa)		

However, this period of political and economic liberalization gradually also led to increase political freedoms in the country. Corruption issues and mismanagement of public funds were increasingly denounced and condemned by national media, and Tanzania's civil society. This more liberalized political context reached its climax in the period right before the 2015 elections. This could be partly explained as well by the fact that, under the presidency of Jakaya Kikwete – from 2005 to 2015 – the CCM became embroiled in many significant corruption scandals, which were virulently denounced in national media and by opposition parties. Denunciation of corruption is not stranger as well to a proliferation of political factions at that time, which were out-competing each other in the scramble for rents, especially in the energy sector. Among the most important was the Richmond scandal over the improper attribution of a contract to a US-based electricity company, which led to the resignation of the government's Prime Minister, Edward Lowassa. Later, in 2014, the Escrow scandal shocked the nation when a multimillion-dollar corruption scheme within the government was exposed. Documents and reports showed that two senior Tanzanian politicians had taken and transferred about US$ 180 million from the Bank of Tanzania into offshore accounts. In addition to forcing the resignation of two senior ministers and of the attorney-general, the scandal implicated many important businessman, politicians and judges (Cooksey, 2012, 2017; *The Guardian*, 2014; Brewin, 2016; *Tanzania Daily News*, 2017). Thus, CCM's tarnished image posed a tangible threat to the party's hold on power, especially regarding the upcoming 2015 elections. Just before the 2015 elections, Kikwete's legitimacy was very weak, and approval ratings of his government were historically low (Roop and Weghorst, 2016). CCM's fear was that it might be the end of its fifty-four years of ruling.

Political factionalism, the 2015 elections and Tanzanian politics under Magufuli

Regarding the 2015 elections, CCM's elites were divided over the nomination of their presidential candidate. Although the party's former Prime Minister, Edward Lowassa, was initially a potential presidential candidate, the CCM ultimately decided against him. The fact that Lowassa had to resign following the Richmond scandal, and the increased popular criticism of the CCM forced the party to identify another potential candidate. The CCM then found its Presidential candidate, John Pombe Magufuli. He had cultivated an honest reputation within the government and by the population for his efficiency and his capacity to 'get things done'. He also 'ran on an anti-establishment ticket of "change", portraying himself as an outsider who was siding with the people against a corrupt elite' (Pedersen and Jacob 2019, p. 14) and promoting a populist and nationalist agenda to restore the country richness and proudness. CCM's strategy was thus settled: nominating 'a virtual unknown to carry it into the presidential election' as a way around growing national criticism and the party's damaged reputation ('CCM springs surprise', 2015). Following the CCM's decision not to make him their presidential candidate Lowassa defected to *Chama cha Maendeleo na Demokrasia* (Chadema), the main opposition party and became its leader. Despite Lowassa's previous implication in the Richmond scandal, he was successful in unifying Tanzanian opposition. Indeed, for the 2015 elections, four opposition parties grouped together under Lowassa's leadership. This opposition coalition was named *Ukawa* and posed the toughest challenge to CCM since Independence.

The 2015 elections were characterized by a high turnout, as 67.34 per cent of voters went to the polls (Roop and Weghorst, 2016, p. 172). On 25 October 2015, the CCM, with Magufuli, won the Tanzanian general election with 58.5 per cent of the vote. Although CCM secured its victory, the competition was historically tight as Chadema managed to secure about 40 per cent of the vote. Nevertheless, the CCM's presidential candidate strategy proved successful in allowing the Party to remain in power (Brewin, 2016, p. 201; Roop and Weghorst, 2016). Yet, once elected, the assumption that Magufuli was the compromise candidate, subservient to the CCM, was immediately thrown into question. Magufuli adopted a strong stance towards corruption, even targeting CCM members. For instance, he started his presidency by arresting several senior government officials for corruption charges and allegations.

[In the year of his presidency] Many heads have rolled. [...] Those who have felt the new intolerance of waste and corruption include the Director General of the Tanzanian Ports Authority, Awadhi Massawe; its Board Chairman, Professor Joseph Msambichaka; and most of the members of the

Board. The head of the Prevention and Combating of Corruption Bureau (PCCB), Edward Hosea, was shown the door, and the head of the Tanzania Revenue Authority (TRA), Rished Bade, his deputy and other senior TRA officials were unceremoniously ousted.

('Push-ups and pushback', 2016)

As substantiated in Chapter 4, this move was not only populist, but also served as an effective political tool to establish Magufuli's political authority within the CCM, thereby disciplining both political elites and the Tanzanian business community. Of course, this ousting process: Magufuli has favoured his business and political friends at the expense of others. However, after his first years as a President, Magufuli relaxed his bulldozer approach and showed more openness to political compromises. As his position within the party was still fragile, he learned to wisely pick his battles. In order to build and maintain his authority within the CCM, he had to be careful about challenging too deeply Tanzania's 'well-established settlement between the business and political elites' ('How real the zeal?', 2015; 'The bulldozer's light tread', 2016). On a more general level, Magufuli's governance was characterized by an increased emphasis on state-led development compared to the more neoliberal approaches of past administrations. Tanzania also took an authoritarian turn. As a matter of fact, Tanzania's fifth government has increasingly closed space for dissent, with the banning of political rallies, the harassment and even arrest of opposition political leaders, the toughening of laws overseeing media, the suspension of several newspapers and radio stations, and the recent passing of draconian legislation such as the 2015 Cybercrime Act, the 2015 Statistics Act and the Electronic and Postal Communications (Online Content) Regulations. The Cybercrime Act criminalizes offenses related to computer and electronic devices, and was used to prosecute opposition politicians, journalists and activists for their online posts deemed critical of Magufuli's governance. The Statistics Acts criminalized the publication of statistics which have not been approved by the government. Illustrative of Magufuli's increasingly undemocratic tendencies, in 2017, during the swearing-in of the new Information Minister, Harrison Mwakyembe, the President directly warned journalists: 'I would like to tell media owners, be careful, watch it. If you think you have that kind of freedom, [it is] not to that extent' (Reuters, 2017).

This was the Tanzanian context when, in 2020, the Covid-19 pandemic took the world by surprise. Tanzania's response was to downplay the effects of the pandemic and Magufuli did not put in place any social distancing, precautionary or containment measures. The President rather advocated natural remedies such as steam inhalation or praying. He was also critical of other countries' containment measures, insisting on keeping the economy open. Moreover, he suggested that Covid-19 was somehow linked to a foreign conspiracy against Africa. For instance, he cautioned people against the Covid-19 vaccine, and further stated that international donations of masks might potentially be used to infect Tanzanians with the virus. He also exerted strict control on media companies over their coverage of the pandemic, issuing fines and suspending their licenses (Nyeko, 2021). In June 2020, Magufuli even publicly declared that Tanzania was free of Covid-19 (*BBC News*, 2020a). Despites Magufuli's claims and the fact that Tanzania stopped reporting Covid-19 data, unofficial reports suggest that coronavirus has claimed many lives in Tanzania as elsewhere in the world. For instance, hospitals have been overwhelmed with patients suffering from respiratory distress, and a surge in deaths attributed to pneumonia has been observed (*BBC News*, 2020b; Thomas, 2021). In addition, Tanzanian travellers have been reported to be highly contaminated with variants of the coronavirus, indicating that the country has potentially experienced important Covid-19 outbreaks (*Washington Post*, 2021). It is against this Covid-19 background that the 2020 elections were held on 28 October 2020.

The 2020 elections and Covid-19

Magufuli's authoritarian tendencies reached their climax prior to the elections. Repression heightened up with Magufuli's open repression on the opposition, military presence, the blocking of international media and external observers. Social media networks were also blocked throughout the country, accessible only through VPN (*Al Jazeera*, 2020; Taylor, 2020). In the words of Aikande Kwayu, a Tanzanian political analyst: 'he [Magufuli] is actually bulldozing everything, laws, human rights, everything' (*France 24*, 2021). Indeed, the Tanzanian 2020 elections were not fair, free or credible. Magufuli won the elections with a more than comfortable 84 per cent of the votes while the main opposition party led by Tundu Lissu – who came back to Tanzania after surviving a gun attack in September 2017 – secured only 13 per cent. In a nutshell, the 2020 elections show that, under Magufuli's presidency, the CCM has forcefully taken back its control over Tanzanian politics.

Unexpectedly, Magufuli, aged sixty-one, died on 17 March 2021, officially from heart complications. Rumours are that he died from Covid-19, ironically from this virus he so virulently denied. With respect to the Tanzanian constitution, the then Vice-President, Ms. Samia Suluhu Hassan, was sworn in as the new President to complete Magufuli's five-year term. Born in Zanzibar, Hassan became Tanzania's first female president. She has a background in statistics and economics and completed her postgraduate studies at the University of Manchester, London. Prior to being Magufuli's Vice-President, she worked as a tourism minister in Zanzibar and was also appointed by Kikwete as a minister of state in the Vice-President's office responsible for union affairs. Since she became President, Hassan has been distancing herself from Magufuli by taking a few significant steps. For instance, she made changes in the CCM: ousting Magufuli's loyalists to strengthen her own faction. She reshuffled the government, fired the head of the tax authority and appointed her own finance and foreign ministers. She also lifted the ban on media and pardoned overs 5,000 prisoners. Regarding the Covid-19 crisis, she has publicly acknowledged it and has formed an expert committee to advise Tanzania on how to best address the pandemic. On the economic side, she has been moving away from Magufuli's nationalist discourse and adopted a more neoliberal approach although she has promised to pursue already ongoing mega infrastructure projects. She pledges on stimulating the economy by revising investment policies, laws and regulations to attract more investors (*The Citizen*, 2021). Yet her authority within the CCM and the government remains fragile and her room for political manoeuvre likely to remain narrow because the government is still crowded with Magufuli's allies (Ombuor and Bearak, 2021).

4

The national political arena. Land policies: Political tools to (re)assert state authority over land

This chapter analyses Tanzania's land discourses and policies in relation to this land rush. I show that there are important discrepancies between the central government's pro-poor and pro-development official narratives and practices. To understand these discrepancies, we need examining the politics inherent to this CAS structuring government officials' interactions. More specifically, this chapter documents how and why Tanzanian state officials seize opportunities opened-up by contingencies – the renewed interest for farmland investments – to (re)shape land policies. I argue that they combine diverse normative rationalities – neoliberal development, capitalist exploitation, state-bureaucratic control, developmental paternalism, political clientelism – to justify institutional innovations that are foremost key to establish their control and power over land management. This creative process strengthens their political authority, which is strategic in capturing the economic opportunities that arise with those new farmland investments. It also justifies contentious political actions.

I illustrate this argument with three recent examples. The first two examples, the discourse of the central state on productive investors and the review process of the National Land Policy, focus on the national level. More specifically, I examine how and why the President and central state officials are designing and implementing new land policies. At the central level, institutional innovations (i.e. the creation of a new Land Investment Unit [LIU], and the revision of the National Land Policy) were ways for the former president – as it was for previous presidents – to legitimize and consolidate his political power, on the national political scene but also within, the CCM. They are also tools to assert central state powers over land management and its territorial authority over the countryside. In addition, Magufuli's discourse and policies on bad investors allowed him to use land dispossession as a political tool to discipline potential political opponents. Illustrating similar dynamics at the local level, the third example examines the local implementation in two regions of the Program for Planning, Surveying, and Land Titling in Tanzania (PPSL). It shows that district officials are also seeking to strengthen their authority through new land policies. Planning and mapping village land, for instance, are authoritative practices that enhance state agents' powers not only towards villagers but also with new investors.

Since Magufuli's death, it is unclear yet what strategy the new President intends to use regarding land management. To my knowledge, there is no indication that Hassan wants to change the institutional arrangements that were put in place by her predecessor.

The apparent convergence of international and national narratives on land policies

Since the 1980s, Tanzania has a liberalized economy and its policies on agricultural development are aligned with neoliberal precepts of mainstream international narratives (see Chapter 2). As highlighted by the National Development Vision 2025, the main policy-framework guiding governmental action, commercial agricultural development through investments will foster agricultural productivity through spillovers and technology transfers. The action plan is thus on boosting the agricultural sector to 'transform the economy towards competitiveness' (The Tanzania Five-Year Development Plan 2011–2015 Planning Commission, President's office, 2012). As argued by Sulle (2016), recent agricultural policies all illustrate this paradigm, such as Kilimo Kwanza (2009), Southern Agricultural Growth Corridor (SAGCOT, 2010), New Alliance for Food Security and nutrition initiative (New Alliance, 2012), Big Results Now (BRN, 2012), and the National Agriculture Policy (NAP, 2013). Most of these policies are rooted within a national framework: Tanzania's National Strategy for Growth and Reduction of Poverty or MKUKUTA.[1] MKUKUTA I and II were in fact agreements over strategic funding of policies resulting from a dialogue undertaken between major donors, international institutions such as the IMF and the World Bank, and the Tanzanian government (Tripp, 2012). Both MKUKUTAs' plan of action for agricultural development prioritized surveying, registering, issuing land titles and reviewing periodically the Land Act and associated laws to make them more inclusive, and 'instituting measures to promote conducive and enabling business environment' (PPSL, 2015, p. 6). Thus, land commodification through land planning and formalization are the established priorities for the envisioned commercial agricultural development.

MKUKUTA II ended in 2015. It was followed by the new National Five-Year Development Plan 2016/17–2020/21 (NFYDP 2016/17–2020/21), which integrated previous MKUKUTA planning frameworks. Regarding land, similarly to MKUKUTA II, the NFYDP 2016/17–2020/21 states that 'the current land policy [...] does not facilitate industrialization', highlighting that land acquisition processes are too costly and lengthy, thereby imposing high transaction costs on investors and deterring new investments. The Ministry of Land often reiterates in various national media the government's commitment to ensure agricultural and economic development and reduce land conflicts through its Ministry's ambitious land titling and land use programme. According to this official narrative, planning, surveying and mapping land in Tanzania is both promoting security of land tenure for citizens and fostering land investments. Moreover, the Ministry of Land has initiated in 2015 the process of drafting a new land policy that officially aims at 'ensuring that all citizens of Tanzania enjoy equitable land rights to enable them to participate effectively in economic development, job creation, and poverty reduction' (The National Land Policy, Official Draft, 2016).

This apparent convergence between national and international discourses on agricultural development is hardly surprising. Indeed, since the 1980s, Tanzania, as a heavily donor-dependent country, has eagerly embraced neoliberal ideas and discourse in a variety of domains including national land policies. The role played by the international structure (institutions and narratives) in shaping African politics and policies should not be overstated though. For the Tanzanian case, scholars have showed that, as a semi-authoritarian state, Tanzania's governance system also displays some enduring ideational features associated to its socialist past, such as the conception of the role played by the state in development and the prevalence of top-down governance practices. This line of argument acknowledges the lasting impact of these historical legacies in current policies (Exner et al., 2015; Haulle, 2015; Greco, 2016; Provini and Schlimmer, 2016). However, although international norms and historical legacies have undoubtedly an influence on the framing of Tanzanian land policies, they are not the only factors that we need to account for. This chapter argues that the process underlying institutional change is much more dynamic: acknowledging actors' agency is important. The first two examples show and describe how Magufuli and top officials from the Ministry of Land draw upon and instrumentalized different narratives to (re)shape land policies (S), a process that allows them to produce their authority and legitimacy.

Talking about productive investors, a clever political strategy: Example 1

Since the arrival in power of Magufuli in October 2015, the need to welcome 'productive' investors has been omnipresent in Tanzanian news. Investors who have acquired land and failed to develop their assets have been publicly criticized by the central government in national media. They are depicted as Machiavellian 'tycoons [...] hoarding big portions of land' thereby impeding the economic development of the country. In a strong statement, the Ministry of Land has declared:

> We will seize all the land pieces, which were legally acquired but had never been developed or are now used other than the prime purpose [...] We cannot allow our people to continue to suffer at the expense of investors [...] There are few people who are not supporting what am doing since I annulled their lands. This will not make me stop; I will continue freezing all the land, which have been abandoned by investors regardless of their status and nationality.
>
> (Mulisa, 2016)

This discursive innovation nuanced the 'welcoming investors' of the international narrative about agricultural development but did not fundamentally question the central government's official commitment to use agricultural FDI to foster socio-economic rural development. In addition, it conveys an image of a very powerful and efficient central state, which can punish investors' deviant behaviour. However, the capacity of the government to act on its discourse is uncertain. The main agency dealing with foreign investors regarding land investments, the TIC, proudly branded as the efficient Tanzanian one-stop shop for foreign investors, suffers from an important lack of financial and human resources. In 2016, there were only two researchers in charge of evaluating viability of investments projects and ensure monitoring (interview research officer TIC, 09.2016). Practically, it is an impossible task given the size of the country and the number of investment projects approved or under evaluation in Tanzania. As a result, TIC's data about agricultural investments is either missing or incomplete. For example, in Rufiji District, according to TIC, three investors have operational investments. Investigating these three investments in the field, I discovered that all information about investors that TIC had provided me was incorrect/inaccurate: all registered investors have left the country and have never managed to start production. Investor X – that I have discussed in Chapter 2 – is a telling example. According to TIC, the company is currently operational and doing well. However, the company had moved three years ago from the address in the TIC file and has no longer a permanent office in Tanzania (Bélair, 2016–17, fieldnotes and observations). In addition, Investor X has never started farming operations despite TIC's claim. In fact, the business is facing several difficulties which affect its ability to be operational, but TIC is apparently unaware of Investor X's issues. So, if the government's main agency handling investors lacks capacity, it is legitimate to wonder if and how the government intends to act upon its discourse on bad investors.

Perhaps, from the standpoint of the state, this is not even a relevant question since such a discourse fulfils a political mission that might be deemed more crucial than questions associated with its pragmatic implications. As argued by Schlimmer (2017b), this discourse is populist and may illustrate the fact that the government is seeking legitimacy by linking its actions to historical and politically salient questions of citizenship and national ownership. Indeed, it helps conveying the image of a strong government committed to protecting its vulnerable local and mostly rural population from the internationally and nationally criticized practices associated to land grabbing. I argue that the political utility of such a discourse is much more subversive. First, the central state's demonization of bad and foreign investors obscures the role it has itself played and continues to play in dispossessing rural communities from their access to land to favour investors and political friends. It is a deliberate misdirection. Second, it provides a rationale for centralizing power over land investments, which is key in asserting political control in Tanzania (Cooksey, 2012; Andreoni, 2017; Jacob and Pedersen, 2018).

For instance, Magufuli took two decisive actions regarding management of land investments since his arrival in power. First, he revoked the appointment of TIC's executive director who was appointed by the previous President in 2013. Second, in May 2016, he created a new Land Investment Unit (LIU), which was put under the purview of the Ministry of Land. Officially, the decision was motivated by the desire to remediate to TIC's lack of efficiency. To clearly understand the impact of these changes, it is helpful to clarify the nature of the previous relationship between these two central institutions. The Ministry of Land is a key institution regarding land management in Tanzania because it is the issuing authority of land titles. Officially, the relationship between TIC and the Ministry of Land should be collaborative since TIC needs to involve the Ministry of Land to get derivative land titles for foreign investors, and the Ministry of Land used to transfer parcels of land available for investments to TIC's land bank. In addition, since the Ministry of Land is responsible for recovering land from commercial investors that have failed to develop their assets, it plays a direct role in managing available parcels of land for commercial development, but was delegating this responsibility to TIC. With the creation of LIU, the Ministry of Land's intention was to directly handle investment projects. In short, TIC's failure to follow up and monitor investors has been pointed out as one of the cause of the commercial underdevelopment of several pieces of land available for investments throughout the country. Therefore, instead of transferring land confiscated by the Ministry of Land to TIC, it has been decided that the Ministry of Land will manage these parcels of land available to investors through LIU (interviews officials TIC and LIU, 09/10.2016). The creation of LIU implies thus an important institutional overlap since the new unit has a similar mandate to TIC. In addition, LIU allows the President to interfere directly and use his discretionary power for land allocation to domestic and foreign investors. For example, in October 2016, Magufuli allocated through LIU 10,000 hectares free of charge to a Tanzanian investor, Bakhresa. This land was confiscated by the Ministry of Land from an unproductive investor in the Coast region. The decision appeared to have been based on the President's perception of Bakhresa as an example of a productive investor. Speaking of the company, he stated: 'you are the best example of businesspeople we want [...] the best taxpayer and you have created many employment opportunities' (Mbashiru, 2016).

This narrative on unproductive investors has led to a significant increase of the President's control over land investments in the country. This new LIU was very active in 2017. According to the Ministry of Land, as of August 2017, about 110 parcels of land have been taken back from unproductive investors across the country (interviews officer LIU, 08.2017). It should be noted here that, at the time of my fieldwork, the Ministry of Land refused to disclose the list of confiscated parcels of land and of investors that have been targeted by this policy on unproductive investments. Moreover, whether investors' land rights are revoked because of their unproductivity remains unclear. There are indications that some of those investors were also considered political threats to Magufuli's regime and needed to be disciplined. The few publicly disclosed cases support this conjecture. For instance, the former Prime Minister Fredrick Sumaye has seen his farms in Dar es Salaam and Morogoro regions being seized by the Ministry of Land. He has publicly claimed that it was politically motivated to force him to return to the CCM (Matandiko, 2017). The case of a previously successful Tanzanian investor, Yusuf Manji, is another example. There was an issue regarding land owned by Manji in Coco Beach, Kigamboni, Dar es Salaam. Apparently, the President wanted to take it back for public use. Even though Manji finally complied and apologized publicly, he initially resisted the presidential directive. His resistance put him in various legal troubles. Not only did the President order directly the revocation of his land rights on his farm in Kigamboni, the following day, the CCM stripped him of his counsellor seat. In addition, the Tanzania Revenue Authority (TRA) closed his offices for unpaid taxes, and he was accused of drug trafficking and other illegal operations. In short, he was disciplined harshly through different state channels. He spent about two months in prison until the Director of Public Prosecutions (DPP) announced that all charges were finally dropped. The exact reasons behind this political harassment remained unclear, as is the exact nature of the issue between this specific investor and the President. It is also difficult to evaluate the extent to which this policy on unproductive investors has been used to this end since a climate of fear was prevailing amongst investors in Tanzania during my fieldwork in 2016–17. Moreover, information on LIU's land confiscations is kept secretive: very few have been made public. Nonetheless, although most investors I met refused to disclose any information on their land holdings because of the politically sensitive context, my interviews reveal that some of them are in precarious situations with the current government. My findings also show that even land holdings and land acquisition projects of successful and established Tanzanian investors are kept on hold by the President himself.

In sum, drawing on diverse discourses and norms that legitimize his actions, Magufuli (re)shaped the institutional structure on land management to strengthen his political authority. The creation of LIU established its political power, on the national political scene but also within his own Party (CCM). Moreover, it ensured the President's control over new investors and new capital. His discourse and policies on unproductive investors legitimized targeted dispossession of land assets. Land management is a crucial political tool in Tanzania: not only to take benefit from land commodification but also to discipline the political and business communities. Given that Magufuli's position within the CCM was still fragile, it seems plausible to assert that he was struggling to constitute and assert its power within the Party. Practices associated with land confiscations played thus a performative role. Magufuli showed that he was not afraid of using all means of the government apparatus at his disposal to discipline potential dissidents or opponents (see discussion on 2015 elections and on political factionalism within the CCM in Chapter 3). Concomitant to these actions, the central state has also initiated another institutional change: the revision of its National Land Policy (NLP). After presenting the legal framework governing land rights in Tanzania, the following section discusses how this new NLP consolidates the central state's territorial authority over the countryside.

Legal framework governing land rights and ownership in Tanzania

As briefly discussed in Chapter 3, in Tanzania, legally, all land belongs to the President: 'all land [...] is public land vested in the President as trustee on behalf of citizens' (National Land Policy 1995, Government of Tanzania, 1995). There are three legal categories of land: general land, reserved land and village land. The Tanzanian land legislative framework includes the Tanzania National Land Policy 1995 which lays the general principles of land management, the Land Act No. 4 1999 which governs general and reserved land and the Village Land Act No. 5 1999 that regulates village land. Reserved lands include national parks, forests and marine environments that are parts of national efforts to conserve wildlife. Village land refers to land which is collectively owned by residents of a given village and is under the authority of the village council. General land is a residual category: everything that is not reserved or village land falls into general land, including land deemed available for investments. Acquiring or leasing land usually involves central agencies (such as the TIC) and the Ministry of Land. In practice, the process is the following: villagers agree, willingly or not, to give up their village land rights, and this parcel of land is transferred permanently to general land. In addition, Tanzanian investors can obtain rights of occupancy on general land. Foreigners, however, can only be granted derivative rights of occupancy. Consequently, they must pass through the TIC which remains legally the ultimate holder of land rights on their behalf.

Drafting a new land policy: Example 2

The process of reviewing the 1995 Land Policy started in August 2015. According to the second draft of this new National Land Policy (hereafter NLP 2018), it was motivated by the desire to adapt policies, programmes and strategies to a changing global context, to bring sustainable local socio-economic development, and to better address challenges that have arisen in the land sector. It also aims at fostering land investments and at expanding the government tax base (NLP 2018, p. xiii). The NLP 2018's ambition is thus at achieving sustainable and inclusive rural development and economic growth. It includes many commendable objectives such as objective 3.2.2 Equitable access of and access to land by all citizens; objective 3.3.2 Secured land rights for agriculture; objective 3.30.2 Gender equality in access to land rights; objective 3.31.2 Secured and protected access to HIV/AIDS affected persons and other vulnerable groups. However, there is no specification in the NLP 2018 on how those objectives will be reached and on the legal recourses available if such legal dispositions are not respected.

In addition, a careful reading of the NLP 2018 content shed doubt on what are the 'real' objectives behind such a policy initiative. There are many indications the NLP 2018 also aims at (re)centralizing land management. First, some statements are inconsistent. For instance, the policy reiterates the importance of decentralizing land administration (policy statement 3.32.3, p. 51). At the same time, it introduces an important change in land administration by stating that village land will be managed by villagers but *under the purview* of a state agent who will oversee planning and mapping processes (policy statement 4.4.2, point iii, p. 55). This change is significant because disempowering villages' authorities (re)centralizes village land management. On paper, villagers will be still administering land but now they will do under the supervision of a state agent, working directly with the District Commissioner (DC). In Tanzania, DCs are directly accountable to central authorities and named by the President himself. Therefore, such a disposition establishes the authority of the central state over village land management, which is in contradiction with the 1999 Village Land Act, which grants this authority to villagers.

Second, the NLP 2018 reaffirms that 'all land [...] is public land vested in the President as trustee on behalf of citizens' and that 'the President may equally acquire land for public purpose or revoke a right of occupancy for breach of conditions' (NLP 2018, p. 8). Regarding foreign land investment, the policy further states that a 'non-citizen or a foreign company cannot be allocated or granted land unless it is for investment purposes. Where the land required for foreign investment is village land, the grant is preceded with approval by the village assembly and consent by the President for the land to be transferred to General Land' (NLP 2018, pp. 7–8). It means that allocation of land for investment purposes will be under the purview of the central state who will ensure the optimal use of land resources (objective 3.6.2,

p. 33). By strengthening the discretionary power of the President regarding land allocation and administration, the NLP 2018 reiterates a disposition that leaves room for ambiguity and interpretation. This has caused in the past several land conflicts and legal issues. Many scholars have denounced the dangers of not defining what is public purpose and the vagueness of the general land category in the 1999 land policies. Furthermore, within the NLP 2018 draft, not only the discretionary power of the President for 'public purpose' is maintained, but there is also the introduction of a new potential loophole with the term 'sustainable agriculture'. For instance, there are the following statements in the section discussing land rights security: 'In collaboration with respective authority, ensure that land suitable for sustainable agriculture is prioritized for food production'; 'Secure rights for all lands of sustainable agriculture' (NLP 2018, section 3.3.3, p. 31). Yet 'sustainable' is defined only in very general terms in the introduction (see on p. x) and will therefore remain subject to interpretation. It is thus unclear whether smallholders' agricultural practices are considered 'sustainable' by the government and which criteria are used to define this so-called sustainability. It might become an important issue as 'unsustainable agricultural practices' may be used to justify villagers' land dispossession.

Third, the policy includes many unsubstantiated statements that are justifying this recentralization of land management. For example, it blames incompetent local authorities for the ineffective implementation of the 1999 land policies. Tanzania's failure to have a good macroeconomic performance is attributed to the 'inadequate assimilation of the national development priorities at the local level' (Tanzania Development Vision 2025, 1999). It also emphasizes that Tanzania has plenty of 'unused land' and that peasants' agricultural activities are unproductive: 'a large part of rural land is economically underutilized' (NLP 2018, p. 42). In short, failure to meet socio-economic development expectations is consistently attributed to villagers' misunderstanding of the central economic priorities regarding land development. In addition to reproduce some of the misleading assumptions of the mainstream international agricultural development agenda (see Chapter 2), such statements share striking resemblances with the long-established paternalistic narrative that has been dominating development conception in Tanzania since Independence.

My contention is that this revision of the National Land Policy, despite all stated objectives, is foremost a process that aims at strengthening the President and the central state's authority over land management and administration all over Tanzania. As I have demonstrated, the NLP 2018 introduces this recentralization cleverly, by drawing on different narratives that help legitimizing it, such as this international narrative on equitable access to land, on the importance of ensuring sustainability to face climate change issues and on the importance of land commodification and formalization for socio-economic development. At the same time, the NLP 2018 reiterates and incorporates paternalistic statements and top-down governance practices associated with Tanzania's socialist past. Therefore, even though NLP 2018 is still a draft and we do not know whether it will be adopted or not, this revision process illustrates well how actors may instrumentalize institutional change to foster their interests and draw on different norms to legitimize their actions. Yet land policies are not only tools instrumentalized by the President and central state officials, as the last example demonstrates. District officials also innovatively use the new conjuncture to strengthen their power over land management. This third example focuses on local officials' practices associated with mapping and planning village land in two different Tanzanian regions, Pwani and Kagera.

Mapping villages or how district officials constitute their authority: Example 3

The Ministry of Land's Program for Planning, Surveying, and Land Titling in Tanzania (PPSL) aims to reduce unplanned settlements, decrease land conflicts, increase the use of land as a collateral for loans among smallholders, and facilitate land administration (registration and revenue collection) (PPSL 2015, p. 4). Regarding village land, PPSL envisages a sequence that starts with providing villages with land-use plans (VLUPs), before issuing titles in the form of a certificate of customary rights of occupancy (CCROs) to villagers. Land-use plans are conceived as tools for planning and guiding land development, and they usually have a ten-year period of validity. The programme explicitly states that processes of planning, surveying and titling rural land will be undertaken in partnership with local communities, thereby 'increasing public awareness on land-related policies, laws, and guidelines', and contributing to local 'capacity building and training' on land management (PPSL 2015, p. 4).

During my fieldwork, I found that villagers are usually involved to some extent in the process of drafting their land-use plan, as the process requires each village to name two representatives to collaborate with the district planner and surveying experts from the district and the Ministry of Land. However, their influence over the process and its outcomes is minimal. The planners and surveyors have the final authority over mapping, leading to practices of consultation that are more procedural than collaborative: villagers are not allowed to significantly contribute to the process or to contest higher authorities. For example, in a village in Pwani region, sunshine at a specific time of the day was traditionally used to identify village demarcations. The village representatives asked the planning team to wait for the right timing for them to correctly identify the boundaries of their village. Their request was refused and therefore, the boundaries were delimited approximately. Unsurprisingly, it led to a problematic land-use map because the identified boundaries were wrong, leading to village land loss. Despite repeated demands from the village for correctives to their land-use map and an explanation of the problem they encounter with the mapping process, villagers were unable to achieve any change. The Ministry of Land resolved the issue by stating that changes are not allowed (interview local leaders Rufiji district, 11.2016). Although every village has specific experiences, I consider this example illustrative of general trends in Missenyi and Rufiji District as I heard similar stories in almost all seventeen villages I visited.

In addition, the Ministry of Land put forward a cadastral mapping of villages that does not necessarily consider historical and local understandings of demarcations. Thus, mapping practices currently undergoing in Tanzania share resemblances to the way villagization was conceived and implemented in the 1970s, therefore demonstrating the lasting impact of socialist rationalities of domination. In fact, Scott's argument (1998) according to which villagization in Tanzania was a large-scale engineering project is still very relevant to understand the way the state is implementing its current land-planning program. Indeed, the Ministry of Land favours an idea of what a developed village should look like, privileging straight boundaries over historical demarcations, thereby leading to villages' land dispossession (interview district official, Missenyi district, 08.2016). For instance, in Kagera region, several villages have ended up losing parts of their land. Among other examples, one of the villages received its land-use plan and village land title in 2015. However, the leaders quickly realized that the boundaries were flawed, and a whole section of their village was missing from the map. The VLUP draws a straight line rather than the curve which was necessary to include this part of the village. Following a village meeting, the village collectively decided to refuse the map provided to them. When the leaders raised the issue with the district and explained why they refused to recognize the validity of their VLUP, district officials threatened them. The district made clear that by refusing to agree with this land-use plan, their village may end up losing all its land. Powerless, the leaders were afraid of the consequences of their resistance. They complied and signed the document, preferring losing a part of their village land than risking losing it all (interview local leaders Missenyi district, 08.2016). According to the district officials I interviewed, conflicts over determined boundaries resulting from the planning process are common issues in the district.

Villages' apparent compliance[2] can here be explained by the inherited socialist, paternalistic and top-down vision of governance that still prevails in Tanzania. Officials at all levels still acknowledge the central government as the uncontested authority over land matters since according to the law 'all land is vested in the powers of the President in Tanzania'. As one district land officer working in Kagera region explained to me:

> The government is trying to involve rural communities in planning and mapping processes, but in the end, the government is the only legitimate authority when it comes to land. If people do not understand what is good for them, the government must [and has the right to] use its power for the public good.
>
> (interviews Missenyi district official, 08.2016)

Therefore, the government should not only provide guidance and a legal framework: if required, it must educate and discipline Tanzanians. This is illustrative of how mapping practices at the local level are influenced by different normative institutions: state-bureaucratic control, developmental paternalism, and neoliberal development. Furthermore, the process is consolidating local officials' political authority. In the cases analysed here, it is through their powers with VLUPs that district officials position themselves towards villagers. As during villagization, planning has a performative function: it is a 'key discursive practice in which the positionalities of officials and peasants were [are] performed and fabricated' (i.e. Schlimmer, 2017a; Engström, Bélair and Blache, 2018). In the current context, district officials' position was somewhat weakened by the 1999 Village Land Act, which decentralized powers over land management to village entities, i.e. the Village Council and the Village Assembly. With the implementation of this mapping program, district and the Ministry of Land officials are thus recreating and performing their identity as experts – using their proclaimed technical expertise as planners and surveyors – to (re)constitute their authoritative position. Thus, district officials used VLUPs not only to establish their control over land management but also as constitutive tools of their authority. Furthermore, (re)constituting their powers over village land offers valuable opportunities to capture and build lucrative relationships with new investors.

The next section examines in detail how district officials constitute their position of authority towards villagers to benefit from the increased commodification of land. I argue that district officials' actions can only be understood by also considering the importance of clientelistic relations of power in Tanzania. They constitute a normative institution that informs and motivates their practices. Investors provide new capital in a country which urgently needs it. A local lucrative business in Tanzania is associated with dynamics of land control and this welcoming of foreign investors. District officials benefit financially at several levels from the arrival of new investors in their area: development levy, taxes, and disguised bribes are paid at different steps during the acquiring land process. Although my analysis is limited to two districts, similar conclusions have been reached in studies of investment projects in Tanzania (Schlimmer, 2017a; Engström, Bélair and Blache, 2018).

Forceful attribution of village land in Rufiji district

Rufiji district, Pwani region, is part of SAGCOT, and thus, one of the most targeted districts for land investments in Tanzania. Numerous investors are looking to acquire village land for their agricultural projects. In addition, most of them are interested in acquiring fertile and cleared land, located near water sources, and therefore find themselves in direct competition with villagers to gain access to this valuable land. In the district, nearly all village land has been surveyed. Out of thirty-eight villages, only four do not have their land certificates, mostly because some boundaries conflicts with neighbouring villages are not solved yet. All villages have demarcated land for investments in their VLUP. Usually, villagers tend to attribute for investment the part of their village land that is less valuable to them, i.e. land that they have not developed or that is currently not used. Since new investors lack local knowledge, they are highly dependent on local state officials when it comes to the process of selecting and acquiring suitable land. This relation with investors empowers district officials and provides them with incentives to benefit financially from their position as village land-use planning authorities. District officials' power allows them to modify the VLUP and demarcate valuable village land as land available for investment when requested by investors. Their involvement and help are not free: district officials charge facilitation fees to investors for their assistance in making the desired land available for investment. For example, in the case of Frontline – an investor in Rufiji district – Walwa (2017, p. 3) reports that district officials have charged the company TSH 25,000 (US$ 15.60) per hectare.

In practice, the process created important confusion at the local level. According to my interviews with villagers and local leaders, the information regarding the location of investments was kept ambiguous during meetings between investors, district officials and villagers. Most villagers assumed that the investor had acquired land in the area demarcated for investment in their VLUP, when in practice the investor had acquired land somewhere else in the village because district officials could adjust the VLUP subsequently. This was the case for all investments projects I investigated where the land transfer had been completed. In addition, my interviews with village leaders and villagers indicate the prevalence of similar dynamics for projects that are still in the process of land acquisition. For one specific case, investors' interests were concentrated in parcels of land located near the Rufiji riverbanks, which is a very fertile area with access to water. For the exact same reasons, it is also where most villagers have historically settled and currently live. Therefore, if this project is carried out, it will entail the displacement and relocation of villagers who never agreed to make this land available for investment in their VLUP. In Rufiji, district officials have innovatively subverted the very function of VLUPs, using them to attribute villages' most valuable land to investors. Instead of providing security of land tenure to villages through their semi-static nature, VLUPs are in practice used as flexible tools to strengthen district officials power over village land, giving them priority access to new possibilities for personal accumulation through third parties' investments.

Direct dispossession through mapping in Missenyi district

Although their interests are similar in Missenyi district, Kagera region, district officials' way of proceeding is different. Missenyi district was not one district prioritized for the PPSL programme. It is a relatively new district which was created in 2007. It comprises seventy-seven villages, and from this, seventy-two villages have been surveyed but none of them have received their VLUP (interview officer Missenyi district, 08.2016). The arrival of Kagera Sugar in 2004, the only large-scale investor in the district, is an important explaining factor. Since Kagera Sugar started operations, land scarcity has become more acute in the district, not because of the company's acquisition of land, but rather because of its contract farming program. A direct consequence of this programme was to attract several local investors, who have decided to produce sugarcane for the company. Since these investors are looking to acquire land, it has increased land scarcity and induced a surge in prices for land in villages surrounding Kagera Sugar (this point is discussed in Chapter 6).

These new dynamics of increased competition for land in the district have opened new accumulation opportunities for district officials (see also Theodory, 2017), especially because of their power position as mapping authorities. However, instead of subverting the function of VLUPs after they have been established, as district officials do in Rufiji, dispossession of land occurs right at the beginning of the mapping process in Missenyi. This way of proceeding is rather advantageous regarding new investments because it frees land while protecting investors at the same time from being involved in conflicts with local populations. The process is also economically motivated. Indeed, in most cases where villages ending up losing land with this process, the contentious missing village land had already been reattributed to local investors by district officials. Missenyi district officials' key role as mapping authorities positions them politically not only towards villagers but also towards new investors. Since they are asserting their political power and authority through their role of mapping experts, investors are now required to obtain the district authorization for all land acquisitions. That was not the case when villages' leaders were the deciding authorities over their village land. To use Fogelman and Bassett's expression (2017, p. 257), official maps are thus 'remaking land as an alienable commodity' and thereby constituting district officials' territorial authority.

Conclusion

This chapter documented how state officials, at central and local levels, cleverly seized new opportunities opened by contingencies – such as the growing investment interest for land in Tanzania, and this international development push to title and map land – to (re)shape the structure (S) of land management. Combining diverse narratives, state officials are crafting land policies in a way that justify centralization of power and contentious political actions. Institutional changes such as the creation of an overlapping institution to manage farmland investments or drafting a new National Land Policy that centralizes powers over land management are helping the Tanzanian state to consolidate its authority at various governance levels. These changes are related to the land rush: investors' increased interest for farmland in Tanzania creates new economic opportunities. Capturing the benefits associated with land commodification is thus at the heart of this Tanzania investment game and of these institutional innovations. Moreover, the examples discussed here illustrate how state officials strengthen their authority over land and contribute to our understanding of how land policies participate to the complex and continuous process of state formation in Tanzania.

Importantly, such dynamics are at the heart of dispossession processes that fuel local grievances against state officials and investors in Tanzania. Regardless of the success and/or failure of new investments, because of the legislative framework governing land rights in Tanzania, Tanzanians lost their village land rights permanently. Such dispossession dynamics are contradicting the socio-economic development narratives that are often associated with agricultural development and investments. This investment game tends to increase land insecurity, and as the next chapters will demonstrate, is far from succeeding in bringing lasting and sustainable socio-economic development at the local level. Also, since the central state is overseeing those investments, villagers are often left without levy and cannot hold investors accountable when they failed to fulfil their promises and obligations. Tanzanian smallholders are thus often left worse-off: losing their land rights without securing any substantial gains from the land rush.

5

Rufiji district, a local political arena. Assessing the role of state brokers

Although Chapter 4 focuses on important political interactions which we need to capture to understand the local impacts associated with new farmland investments, such an understanding is not sufficient. The state is not a unitary actor, and its authority is contentious and limited. Therefore, as Migdal (1997, 2001) suggests, considering how national policies and discourses are transformed by actors throughout the implementation process is crucial to understanding the impact of their interactions, and governance practices on local communities. Addressing Migdal's advice, this chapter shows that we should not overestimate the capacity of central state officials to implement central policies. Given the fragmented and contentious nature of authority, state intermediaries also play an important role in negotiating central institutions and policies to foster their own interests. More specifically, this chapter compares the involvement of two Tanzanian state agencies in land acquisition in Rufiji district, in the context of the central government's new strategy on productive investors. As already mentioned, Rufiji district is one of the most targeted districts for land investments in Tanzania (Figure 5.1 maps the investments projects of the district at time of my fieldwork).

An earlier version of this chapter was published in the *Journal of Modern African Studies*. See Bélair, Joanny. (2018) 'Land Investments in Tanzania: Assessing the Role of State Brokers'. *Journal of Modern African Studies*, 56 (3), pp. 371–394. © 2018 Cambridge University Press, 'Reprinted with permission'.

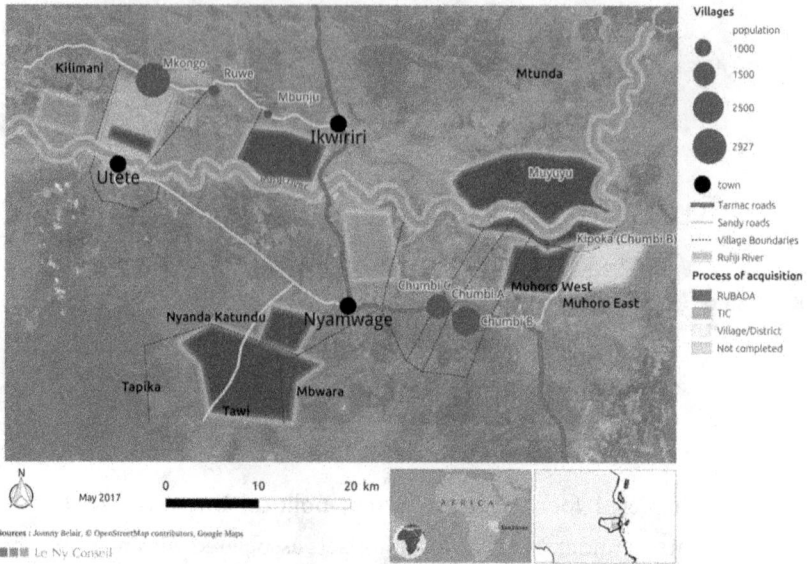

Figure 5.1 Ongoing farmland investment projects, Rufiji district, 2016–17.
Sources: Joanny Bélair, copyright 2017 OpenStreetMap contributors, Google maps; created by Le Ny Conseil.

In this chapter, I unpack bureaucrats as a group of actors to analyse flows of power within the state. My analysis shows that the central state's weak infrastructural power and resulting lack of local knowledge, and, conversely, local bureaucrats' possession of these valuable resources, reverses the flow of power from local to central. Therefore, this chapter documents how intermediaries exert their agency in renegotiating the structure in Rufiji district. It illustrates this argument with two distinct examples. First, I examine how district officials started partnering and protecting unproductive investors from central state's dispossession to maintain and protect their clientelistic relationship with investors. Second, I document how Rubada, a state agency, redefined itself and its mandate in one of the most targeted regions for land investments. In addition to using its position of power to exploit village leaders' lack of knowledge, Rubada started voluntarily misleading central authorities on investors to facilitate land acquisition processes and preserve its intermediary position with investors in the district. Lastly, Rufiji cases also underscore the local pervasive effect of these competitive and subversive interactions between central state officials and bureaucrats. Instead of protecting vulnerable populations, central monitoring process fosters institutional innovations that protect local bureaucrats' opportunities for accumulation with investors, to the detriment of local populations. Moreover, the quasi-systematic presence of local bureaucrats[1] as intermediaries is key in understanding the relation investors develop with local communities. Because of the presence of state brokers, interactions between villagers and investors are almost inexistent: investors delegate to intermediaries the negotiation process. This exclusion of village authorities is likely to generate conflictual dynamics at local level and may impede the investor's capacity to start operations.

Reversing the flow of power in a context of limited state power or how district officials used to capitalize on their local knowledge

As explained in Chapter 4, in theory, investors who want to acquire rights to land in Tanzania should pass through TIC. Based on their needs, TIC should allocate them available and suitable parcels of land from its land bank. However, because TIC's land bank is incomplete, this process is often reversed in practice. Instead of passing through TIC to find suitable land, investors rather identify the land they want to acquire and used TIC only to formalize their land rights. TIC thus depends on local authorities to find and demarcate investors' requested land. It is also local authorities that oversee informing, consulting and securing villages' approval before transferring the village land to the general land category. Therefore, TIC's lack of capacity has put the agency in a relation of dependency with local authorities. TIC depends on them regarding investment projects because they are the ones in the field, and they have a much better understanding of the specificities of the local context. This dependency has significantly empowered district officials, creating opportunities to foster their material interests with investors. The process generates revenues for district officials because of their involvement in several steps – land identification, land mapping, organization of consultations with villagers, etc. – for which they asked investors' direct financial contribution. It also creates an obvious conflict of interest. District authorities have a direct material interest in satisfying investors and in concluding the land deals with the concerned villages even though it means disregarding village authority on land rights (i.e. even though they did consult the villages, villages' approval or refusal was inconsequential). In all three acquisitions, I investigated involving TIC in Rufiji district, concerned villages – both village leaders and villagers – were opposed and refused the land deals, but the land transfers were nonetheless approved and completed.

My analysis shows that excluding village administrations is likely to create conflictual dynamics at the local level, and potentially, may impede investors' capacity to become operational. Indeed, this way of proceeding generates important confusion at the local level. Some villagers are not even aware that their land has been leased to an investor. Even when they are informed, because they were excluded from the negotiation, they lack knowledge about the investor, and it prevents them from holding investors accountable and monitoring expected benefits. For instance, villagers and local leaders are usually denied access to the contract and the terms of the agreement. Even basic information, such as the name of the investor and his contact details, are kept secret. In fact, villagers use nicknames to speak about these investors, which illustrates their lack of information. The process also creates tensions between local populations and investors. An investor that I will refer to as Investor A, for the purpose of anonymity, is a representative case in this regard. The company acquired 3,060 hectares of land for maize and rice production in 2005. TIC approved the land transfer without consulting the village. The village was eventually convinced that the investor's presence would contribute to village development. The investor promised several things to villagers: to provide material for schools and to build classrooms, to expand the health centre, to ensure access to electricity and to provide employment to villagers. None of these promises was fulfilled (interviews local leaders Rufiji, 11. 2017).

A first conflictual issue emerged with the compensation process. Since the land acquired was already occupied by farmers, the arrival of the investor required their displacement. According to the Tanzanian law, in such cases, farmers are entitled to receive compensation for their land. Displaced farmers were offered in 2005 a compensation amount. The company gave the compensation amount to TIC, and TIC delegated the responsibility to compensate farmers to the district. Thus, the district, on behalf of the company, offered farmers TSH 45,000 (US$ 20.14) for every five acres (about 2 hectares) without any compensation for the crops they had already planted or their mango trees. This offer was so low that most farmers were insulted and refused. Nothing happened afterwards: apparently, the district kept the money, and it was the end of it. This compensation process led to frictions between the company and the villagers. On the one side, villagers resented the company for what they perceive as an unfair treatment. On the other, the company claimed that it was a victim as well since they gave a fair amount to compensate farmers directly to TIC (interview Company A, 11.2016). Although the role played by the district and TIC in this compensation is unclear, the fact remains that those compensation issues negatively affected the relationship between investors and farmers.

Moreover, the process of starting agricultural production generated conflicts. Since villagers were not consulted and properly informed about the land acquisition, boundaries between the land owned by the investor and the villagers remained blurred. In the case of Investor A, this confusion over boundaries created problems. After acquiring the land, the company started its operations and planted a small area with maize – between 300 hectares and 700 hectares. However, its first harvest was a loss because, according to the company, about two-third of it was stolen by villagers. Villagers denied this accusation. According to them, the company pretended to cultivate its land but was in fact cultivating the plots that had already been prepared by villagers. So villagers were not stealing from the company but harvesting their own crops. Although what really happened is uncertain, the conflict escalated to the point where one person working for the company shot some farmers apparently caught stealing crops, and one of them got a bullet in the leg. Subsequently, the company lost all local credibility. These combined tensions drove the investor to stop production, and the land was abandoned one year later, in 2006. The investor left his farming equipment in the village, but never came back himself. As this discussion illustrates, the tendency of district officers to exclude villages from land acquisition negotiations tends to generate conflicts between investors and villagers. Villagers, being ignored, lack information about the investor and the location of his investment, thereby creating local conflicts over land use and boundaries. Also, because compensation processes are often problematic, villagers tend to resent the company for not compensating them properly even though the company may not be the sole responsible party for insufficient compensation. In the end, it may have important consequences for investors by impeding their capacity to start operations, as was the case with Investor A.

With the institutional changes regarding land administration and policies that Magufuli implemented (see discussion in Chapter 4), the game has changed at the local level. However, not necessarily in the direction intended by central authorities. The centralization process of land management and the creation of the Ministry of Land's LIU not only has disempowered TIC, but also has weakened the position of district officials. Indeed, this centralization allows the central state to bypass district authorities and proceed with investors directly in a typical top-down process. Consequently, district officials lost their upper hand in the local investment game: this institutional change significantly reduced their capacity to benefit materially from new investors. However, as the next section claims, district officials were very innovative in finding new ways of fostering their material interests, especially in areas where the state has limited infrastructural power.

Institutional change and central monitoring: Forcing local officials to innovate to safeguard their material interests with investors

District officials: Gaming the system and protecting unproductive investors

'For us, they [Investor B] will do nothing. It is just a show', *Rufiji farmer, 2016*

Even though its new strategy allows the central state to bypass district authorities regarding land acquisitions, central authorities still rely on district officials to follow up on the productivity of existing investors. This relation of reliance allows district officials to preserve their power with current investors. In addition, Magufuli's pledge to fight unproductive investors created a climate of fear among investors. Consequently, some investors who have undeveloped assets are afraid of losing their land rights. This situation gives district officials a new and interesting edge with these unproductive investors. Using two examples in Rufiji district – Investor B and Investor C – I draw attention to how the reality on the ground contradicts district officials' discourse on investors' operationalization of projects. I argue that this discrepancy can be explained by considering district officials' strategy to benefit materially from investors, or put differently, the structuring impact of clientelistic relations of power on actors' interactions at the local level.

The case of Investor B

Investor B acquired 3,000 hectares in Rufiji in 2004 to grow sugarcane. The company is local and owned by Tanzanians. It acquired the land directly from the village and this acquisition forced the displacement of about fifty to sixty families. The district was involved in a compensation process that was highly contentious.[2] Furthermore, the company did not respect the development promises it made, never started operations and eventually disappeared from Rufiji. Consequently, several farmers felt they were treated unfairly, and the company acquired a bad reputation locally. However, in 2016, the owner of the company came back to Rufiji district. According to district officials and local leaders, Investor B has shown a renewed interest and is now committed to starting its commercial operations by clearing its land to prepare for cultivation. In short, the company is depicted as a promising investor who will soon become productive. Yet villagers show serious doubt about this official narrative. They believe Investor B is primarily motivated to be active because he is afraid of the President's threat regarding unproductive investors. Thus, they attribute Investor B's motivation to the fear of losing its rights to the land. My field observations tend to support villagers' interpretation. Instead of using tractors as it could be expected in similar cases of commercial agricultural ventures, Investor B made an agreement with the village chairman to hire youths to clear his land by hand. The least we can say is that this way of proceeding for such a big parcel, 3,000 hectares (7,400 acres), is far from being optimal. In the words of one farmer: 'they [the youths hired by the Chairman on behalf of the company] use primitive tools such as *panga* [machete]. To us, they [Investor B] will do nothing. It is just a show' (interview farmer Rufiji, 12.2016). Although Investor B's real motivations remain subject to speculation, the significance of this example lies in showing the process through which the company has established partnerships with district officials and local leaders to protect itself from central state's dispossession. When I asked district officials about

Investor B, they depicted him as being committed and operational. I interpret this discourse as one that aims at protecting the company, and district officials' interests with it. Without a doubt, officials are aware, as are villagers, that Investor B's current land clearing operations are seriously contradicting his claim and commitment to become commercially productive.

The case of Investor C

Investor C provides another illustrative example.[3] The company has acquired about 5,000 hectares in Rufiji for rice cultivation in 2015 through TIC. The process of this deal was particularly top-down and secretive. At local level, the process of acquisition was so obscure that both villagers and leaders do not know how the company acquired this land (interview land rights monitor Rufiji, 11.2016). The location of the land acquired itself is surprisingly imprecise in official documents: the affected villages are not identified (interview research officer TIC, 09.2016). Operationalizing agricultural operations on this specific land is problematic for many reasons. First, the land acquired is in a very remote and undeveloped area of the district. To reach it, which I did, one needs to cross a small artisanal bridge over the Rufiji River and then to drive about twenty-eight kilometres on a narrow, sandy road. Clearly, lack of infrastructural development is challenging for any investor who wants to develop commercial agriculture. There is no electricity, no water and the roads are not sufficiently developed to allow regular transportation. Moreover, before being able to cultivate this land, it would require a fair amount of investment. As I saw when I visited this investment site, the land is an uncleared and wild bush, except for a tiny part where the investor brought a container, dug a well and built the guard's house. In addition, since Investor C's land has shared boundaries with the Selous Game Reserve, the presence of wild animals – elephants, lions, monkeys, hippopotamuses – is likely to disrupt agricultural activities. Unsurprisingly then, the investor has not done much except for enlarging a few kilometres of the road leading to his land and establishing a precarious base camp (see Figures 5.2–5.5). Moreover, it appears that all operations have stopped since February 2016.[4]

Despite these facts, district officials that I interviewed in November 2016 insist on how this investor is productively engaged in this agricultural venture. According to them, the company is committed to being operational soon, and

Figure 5.2 Investor C, path to access the site. Photographer: Joanny Bélair

Figure 5.3 Investor C, container on site. Photographer: Joanny Bélair

Figure 5.4 Investor C, the guard's house. Photographer: Joanny Bélair

Figure 5.5 Investor C, overview investment site. Photographer: Joanny Bélair

currently active in developing the road to reach its land to start agricultural production (interview official Rufiji District, 11/12.2016). This contradiction between my field observations and district officials' discourse is striking. I concluded that protecting this investor from central state's dispossession threat may explain this discrepancy. District officials are more concerned about protecting their interests with this investor than by his eventual capacity to become productive. This would explain why they continue praising the investor's commitment despite being aware of the major challenges to develop agricultural activities on this land anytime soon.

To conclude, under Magufuli's presidency, the central state has put in place a new strategy to increase its control over and foster 'productive' land investments. In Rufiji, it created an institutional overlap which has sidelined district elites and reduced their opportunities for accumulation with investors. However, since the state has weak infrastructural power, it still relies on them to monitor and follow up on investors. I demonstrated that district officials used this power to foster their own material interests. By offering protection against the central state's threat of dispossession, district officials innovated by proposing a new valuable administrative service to unproductive investors: though fragmented and incomplete, data suggest that they may have lied to central government officials to cover up investors' unproductivity. This innovation fosters district officials' material interests because it creates and establishes their usefulness to investors, who must financially compensate them for their assistance (mostly in the form of disguised bribes). Besides this, the centralization strategy of the central state has also led it to monitor closely some local state agencies dealing with land investors in Rufiji. The next section analyses the local impacts of this new central monitoring. I argue that it has a pervasive local effect. Instead of protecting vulnerable populations, it fosters institutional innovations that aim to protect local officials' opportunities for accumulation with investors.

Ambiguous at best, illegitimate at worst: How an agency can reinvent itself as a land broker

Rubada, a state agency that redefined itself and its mandate in one of the most targeted regions for land investments, provides a fascinating illustration of the consequences of the state's lack of capacity on policy implementation. To apprehend the complexity of the CAS which structures Rubada's interactions with other state actors, investors and local populations, historical contextualizing is needed. Rubada, or the Rufiji Basin Development Authority, was a national agency that was established in 1975 by Parliament Act No. 5. Broadly defined, its first mission was to promote, regulate, coordinate and facilitate all development activities in the Rufiji Basin. Rubada was created amid an optimistic development buzz in the Rufiji region with the ambitious Stiegler Gorge Project. It is worth noting that this narrative about the tremendous potential of the Rufiji basin for socio-economic development has been part of the national narrative since the colonial period. Numerous ambitious development projects[5] have been undertaken in the region in hope of taming the Rufiji River for commercial irrigation or generating hydroelectricity. Rubada's initial mandate was thus to coordinate Tanzania's partnerships with international donors and institutions for the development of Rufiji region (Hoag, 2003, p. 183). However, in the end, all these ambitious development projects failed. The implementation of the structural adjustment programme and economic liberalization at the end of the 1980s marked the end of this era of large-scale projects with the abandonment of the Stiegler Gorge Project.[6] As a direct consequence, the mission of Rubada became unclear, but the agency was not dismantled. The turn towards privatization at the end of the 1990s, and the new focus on attracting investors to promote agricultural development provided new opportunities for Rubada. Echoing what neoinstitutionalists call 'institutional stickiness', Rubada officials found a way of reinventing their agency and justifying its existence. In fact, they broadened its mission (Rubada, 2013, p. 4). A wider conception of Rufiji development was put forward, in which the focus on the Rufiji River was replaced by a focus on land. Fostering land investments and attracting new investors in Rufiji region became in practice Rubada unofficial mandate. Yet, because this reorientation was never properly officialized by the central government, the agency's legitimacy remained fragile at both local and central government levels. At worse, Rubada was perceived illegitimate; at best, ambiguous.

Nevertheless, Rubada managed to become a very attractive agency for investors since it started acting as a broker to deal on their behalf with villages, the district and the different ministries. The agency was relatively successful in branding itself as the turnkey agency for land investments in Rufiji district until the outburst of the 2015 corruption scandal with investors. In April 2015, senior officials of Rubada were put under investigation over the disappearance of TSH 3.2 billion of development funds (roughly US$ 1.5 million). According to the report, investors' money was not channelled through Rubada accounts: 'the officials received TSH 2.7 billion from investors who wanted to work in various projects in the basin, but only TSH 714 millions was tracked to Rubada's accounts' (Mwalimu, 2015). Swindled investors never got the land they paid for, and their money simply vanished. Subsequently, the relationship between the central government and the agency became strenuous as top officials began ostracizing Rubada. For instance, its number of employees was diminished drastically: from about 500 employees in the 1990s, the agency had less than 50 in 2017. Moreover, since 2015, the central government stopped funding it. Rubada's offices in Dar es Salam fell into decrepitude, a situation which is a telling contrast with TIC's and the Ministry of Land's LIU newly renovated offices. In addition, to deal with Rubada, the central government directed a close monitoring of Rubada's activities by the Ministry of Land. For instance, the agency must be accompanied by district officials to every meeting with villagers, and their presence is required during negotiations and villages general assemblies. In addition, the Ministry of Land had sent delegates to every village which had signed a contract involving Rubada to validate whether the villages have consented or not to those land investments (interview district officials, Rufiji District, 11/12.2016). This central oversight aimed to ensure that the agency is carrying out its activities with investors properly. Nevertheless, Rubada has remained a very active actor in land investments in Rufiji district, especially since facilitating land acquisition for companies became its only way to generate new revenues. In 2017, the agency was involved in about twenty investment projects. While most of them were still in the preliminary phases of land acquisition, some were at the Ministry of Land, waiting for the completion of the land transfer process (interview liaison Rubada, 11.2016).

Subversion of central monitoring

Even if Rubada lost 90 per cent of its staff in the last decade or so, Rubada officials have an extensive local knowledge of Rufiji district – the agency has been active there for over forty years – and therefore, it does not rely on district officials as TIC does. In practice, when it comes to land acquisitions, Rubada arranges meetings directly with village leaders. Villages leaders are thus always involved in the negotiation and can establish their conditions for the lease of their land. Yet, while such a process empowers village leaders, we should be careful to claim that it is more inclusive of villagers. My field observations suggest that each village in Rufiji district has its own power dynamics, and the result depends on the leaders' relations with the villagers and the nature of consultative mechanisms. I noticed that some leaders favour very transparent processes and villages assemblies are called to openly discuss the investor, the development conditions to be met and the possible advantages of this investment for the community. The discussion and the final decision to lease land or not is thus taken in a concerted and relatively democratic way. However, in other villages, leaders use their position of authority to negotiate privately with Rubada and investors. They keep these transactions secret and refuse to answer the questions of villagers during the meetings. Therefore, these villagers are often not aware of their land having been leased, have no information about the investor and do not know the terms of the contract. In practice then, for land acquired in this fashion, it is highly likely that the local outcomes of land deals will be similar to the ones observed with TIC or LIU.

Before being centrally monitored, Rubada used to collaborate with the district to make sure that land was leased to investors, with or without villages' approval. For instance, in one specific village that I visited, the leaders were approached by Rubada and an investor in 2013. The collective decision was to refuse the investor's request for land for two reasons. First, the land the investor wanted to acquire was bigger than the land available for investors in the VLUP. Second, the village was suspicious of Rubada. They distrusted the agency: 'We don't recognize Rubada's authority, and we don't want to deal with them. From what we know, Rubada's mandate is to help developing the Rufiji River, but it is not what they do. They tend to partner with investors and to not protect people' rights' (interview local leaders Rufiji, 12.2016). Regardless of the village's clear opposition, these leaders learned accidentally while they were at the district office that their land was leased to this investor after all. It means that Rubada ignored the village's decision and colluded with district officials to proceed with the land transaction. However, as part of its close monitoring of Rubada's activities, the Ministry of Land has revised all land deals involving Rubada in Rufiji district. In some instances, it led to acknowledge the illegality of some land transactions and to recognize villages' authority and land rights. The case of this village illustrates the outcome of this central follow-up and monitoring. When the villagers learned that their land was leased despite their refusal, they were shocked. They wrote a letter to the Ministry of Land in 2013 to inform it that their rights have been denied by the district and Rubada, and that they, as villagers, considered this transaction illegal. The villagers themselves never got an answer. Nonetheless, according to my interviews with both Rubada and the district, the village's refusal was acknowledged by the Ministry of Land during its revision of the land transactions involving Rubada. Consequently, the transaction was invalidated, and the village finally kept its land rights.

Yet this outcome appears exceptional. In fact, the Ministry of Land's primary goal is to monitor Rubada to avoid a new corruption scandal with investors. Most of its monitoring on land deals involving Rubada were procedural and conducted only with villages' executive committee, and selected leaders. Thus, the monitoring process itself does not deal with the issue of local leaders who have sold village land on villagers' behalf without properly informing or consulting them. In short, the process overlooks consequences of asymmetrical power within villages. Nevertheless, it puts pressure on Rubada that could not ignore anymore decisions made by villagers. In addition, the agency is under a lot of financial pressure as the central government has cut off its operational funding. Concretely, as I explain below, it forced Rubada to innovate to protect its interests with investors in a context where the agency must secure villages' consent before being able to proceed with the land transfer for investment.

In practice, Rubada started to use its position of power to exploit village leaders' lack of knowledge and of education regarding their land rights and legal proceedings. Most of village leaders I have interviewed do not know that once their land is transferred to the category of general land, it is gone forever. Villagers usually assume that if the investor is not productive, they will be able to get back their land rights, which is not the case. The Tanzanian legal framework does not transfer back general land to village land. Moreover, villagers lack information about the market value of their land and assets, the laws governing their land rights and the compensation process. Since Rubada's main source of revenue is its services as a broker for investors, it has a direct interest in satisfying investors and finding the land they request for their investments, even though it might imply lying to village leaders. For example, Rubada will agree to certain conditions with the village leaders but those conditions will not be included in the official contract with the company. Concretely, numerous villagers have told me that one trick used by Rubada is to write down a bilingual version of the contract. The content of the Kiswahili contract will include villages' requests while the English one – which is used as the official and legally binding contract –

will not. This way Rubada can secure villages' approval by agreeing to all their demands regarding the investor's acquisition, without imposing any constraining development conditions on the investor.

Rubada is not only tricking villages to secure its interests, but it is also voluntarily misleading central authorities to facilitate land acquisition processes. For example, since 2011, Rubada has been officially working with two different companies that are looking to acquire land for sugar production: Investor D and Investor E. Yet these two companies are in fact the same. Rubada and the company's director were afraid that they were asking too much land at once and the Ministry of Land might refuse to allocate such a large area to only one investor – it represents over 25,000 hectares. It is why they created two businesses to avoid suspicion and facilitate the process to obtain land titles (interview Rubada 09.2016, interview Rubada liaison Rufiji 11.2016). The district was complicit in this case. Moreover, the fact that the company has been struggling financially and does not have the financial capacity to develop such an ambitious project does not appear to be a concern for Rubada or the district but should be since it might impede the investor's capacity to be productive. This shows that the central state strategy to foster productive investments has not been internalized by these bureaucrats. Their interest lies instead in the perspective of short-term material gains from their partnership with new investors. Although it can be argued that local officials' actions and interests may not be that subversive and rather resulting from their lack of capacity, my observations in the field contradict this argument. In Rufiji district, local officials are omnipresent and exert strict control over activities within their territory. District officials' constant reluctance to allow me to visit sites of land investments, recurrent inconsistencies between their discourses on investors and the reality on the ground, the law of secrecy regarding investors, and villagers' perceptions and observations support my hypothesis.

Central monitoring has thus direct consequences on the way a local state agency conducts its activities regarding land investments. However, empirical investigation of these effects is necessary to understand how bureaucrats alter these policies during the implementation process. As illustrated in this case, local officials innovated to promote their interests with investors, even though it implied voluntarily misleading and tricking both village and central authorities. Moreover, my analysis highlights that including villages administrations within processes of acquisition is not sufficient to avoid conflictual dynamics between villagers and the investor. This finding points out the crucial importance of acknowledging power dynamics within villages, and, more specifically, leaders' accountability to villagers, to analyse the nature of the potential relationship between investor and villagers. Although Rubada's presence in Rufiji had lasting impacts in the district, its power over farmland investments in the region came to an end when the central government decided to dismantle the agency in September 2017. Its remaining employees were transferred to the Ministry of Agriculture. How the central government is intending to honour Rubada's contractual obligations with investors has not been publicly disclosed.

Conclusion

Based on my empirical findings in Rufiji district, this chapter first showed that the central state's weak infrastructural power may reverse the flow of power, empowering local bureaucrats towards their counterparts. I argued that the fragmented and contentious authority in Tanzania can impact power relations in the field of land deals. My analysis reiterates the importance of recognizing that the hegemonic project of many African states is contentious, dynamic and incomplete (Mandani, 1996; Ferguson and Gupta, 2002, p. 982). Furthermore, it shows that investigating empirically how local actors transform central structuration processes remains highly relevant to understand governance practices in Africa (Mandani, 1996).

In this chapter, I unpacked the local CAS to study how intermediaries have innovatively seized opportunities to subvert central directives, thereby modifying the local structure, which in turn affected their interactions with other actors at the local and central governance levels. Demonstrating that Tanzanian central authorities lacked capacity, I emphasized the dependency that exists between them and local bureaucrats. Because central state officials were dependent on local officials' knowledge, the latter found themselves in position of power which they used to foster their material interests with investors, and their political interests with local populations. As documented in this chapter, in Rufiji district, actors' interactions between levels are mostly competitive and subversive. The nature of this relationship between officials at central and local levels further explains the local impacts associated with new farmland investments that I have observed at the local level. Yet, as the dismantlement of Rubada shows, the central state may emancipate itself from such relations and discipline an agency when its actions are way out of line.

This chapter also indicated that, rather than protecting vulnerable populations, central monitoring might foster institutional innovations that aimed at protecting local bureaucrats' opportunities for accumulation with investors. The fact that local officials acted as state brokers damaged the relationship investors developed with local communities. It generated confusion because local communities were not consulted and lacked information about new investment projects. Being excluded from the negotiation process, the local population tended to resist investors. As a result, conflictual dynamics emerged when these investors started operations. Therefore, bypassing local communities is consequential: it might even impede the capacity of the investor to start operations. At the same time, competitive interactions between central and local governance levels also open possibilities for local communities to protect and safeguard their land rights. But, and importantly, this outcome is contingent on the nature of actors' interactions at the micro-level. It is possible only if local leaders favour transparent governance procedures and are accountable to villagers.

Missenyi district, a local political arena. The impact of protected domestic markets and clientelistic relations

This chapter adopts a local perspective and focuses on one specific and local investor, Kagera Sugar. Regularly cited by the Tanzanian government and the country's press as a success story, Kagera Sugar is currently expanding its operations. Its parent company, Tanzania-based Superdoll, acquired rights to about 25,000 hectares of land in 2004,[1] making Kagera Sugar the largest investor in the Kagera region's Missenyi district. Through substantial infrastructure investments, Superdoll has successfully positioned Kagera Sugar as one of the key players in the Tanzanian sugar industry. This chapter highlights the role of clientelistic relations in shaping production activities and local practices. It shows that actors' political interactions between central and local levels are not always subversive or competitive (as discussed in Chapter 5), they can also be collaborative and interdependent. This interdependency is key because it became the condition that underlies actors' position of authority in this local CAS. Furthermore, although this chapter illustrates how actors exert their agency to subvert or modify the structure to foster their interests, it also evidences that not all actors have the same capacity to influence it. There are structural inequalities in the distribution of power. As a result, it is primarily actors who hold enough power capital – political elites, investors

An earlier version of this chapter was published in World Development in 2021. See: Bélair, J. (2021) 'Farmland investments in Tanzania: The impact of protected domestic markets and patronage relations', *World Development*, 139, pp. 1–9. doi:10.1016/j.worlddev.2020.105298.

and government officials – who can renegotiate the structure to further their political and material interests. Marginalized actors, because of their limited political capital, such as migrant workers, women and youths are often left out of this negotiation game, with very little leeway to influence the structure.

The chapter is divided into three sections. The first discusses the direct socio-economic impact of the company's operations, especially its role in promoting local socio-economic development. However, this direct impact proves to be both limited and uneven. Through an analysis of the broader impact of the company's arrival in the district, the second section provides a deeper understanding of the forces at play. Clientelistic relations play a particularly important role in shaping the local effects of farmland investments, especially in cases where the investor operates within a protected domestic market. I therefore discuss the importance of the sugar industry to Tanzanian politics and how Kagera Sugar secures political protection and preferential treatment through clientelistic relations at the national level, allowing the company to secure its monopoly over sugar production and distribution in the region. Finally, the third section looks at how Kagera Sugar helps shape the agrarian political economy by fostering similar clientelistic relations at the local level. Both the company's contract farming scheme and the politicization of land formalization provide examples of this phenomenon. Furthermore, this political dimension reinforces existing dynamics of social differentiation, creating winners and losers at the local level.

Kagera Sugar: How do peasants cope

During the colonial period, some of the lands that have since been acquired by Kagera Sugar were granted to an Indian investor and developed for sugar production. When operations were nationalized after Independence, productivity remained low due to mismanagement and corruption, as well as a lack of maintenance and funding (interview with Chief of Operations, Kagera Sugar, 08.2016). The state-owned sugar factory was bombed during the Tanzania-Uganda War of 1978–9 and was completely abandoned in the 1980s, remaining idle until its privatization and sale in 2004. During the intervening years, nearby communities made use of the abandoned lands, thereby acquiring occupancy rights under the law. However, the government failed to properly compensate these communities when it sold the land to Kagera Sugar.

Nevertheless, the company has been largely successful in maintaining peace with its new neighbours. On the one hand, villagers have been eager to negotiate with the company to secure benefits from what was previously government land. On the other hand, the company has shown a commitment to building good relationships with surrounding communities. According to my interviews, the few land conflicts that arose following the company's arrival were quickly and peacefully resolved. Superdoll has also invested heavily in local infrastructure projects through financial and in-kind contributions, while creating jobs and fostering social development in nearby communities. Company facilities provide villagers with access to quality health care, clean water and primary education. And in addition to providing direct employment at the factory and on its plantations, Kagera Sugar negotiates farming contracts through an outgrower scheme. In 2016, the company gave me a guided tour of its factory, plantation sites and main buildings. My guide eagerly showed me the nice houses provided to skilled workers and managers, while emphasizing Kagera Sugar's commitment to the well-being of its employees. After a five-star meal at the company restaurant, I also visited the hospital, primary school and new mosque. Company staff, as well as residents of nearby villages, can use these facilities at little or no cost. The overall message seemed to be that beyond competitiveness, efficiency and technological improvements, the company was also focused on providing good working conditions, retaining employees and maintaining good relations with surrounding communities.

However, a closer examination of working conditions at Kagera Sugar paints a much more nuanced picture. In fact, most local people can only access lower-paying jobs, such as cane-cutting or seeding. The few higher-paid managerial or professional positions available require not only a diploma, but also political ties to company officials (interviews farmers and villagers from nine villages, Kagera region, 2016–17). Rather than the nice houses I visited on my tour, most workers live in slum-like labour camps, isolated in the middle of the plantation. They build houses with whatever materials they can find. Working conditions are harsh and salaries are extremely low. Local people can tell when someone starts at the company because entry-level workers 'tend to slim up very quickly'. The company transports workers between different parts of the plantation using big open trucks, similar to the vehicles used for transporting cattle. These journeys are not only uncomfortable, but also dangerous, due to the fights and knife attacks that frequently occur. Women are particularly vulnerable. They face sexual harassment, verbal abuse and sometimes even threats of rape (fieldnotes and observations 2016–17).

It is therefore no surprise that Kagera Sugar struggles to recruit workers for low-skilled jobs (interview human resources manager Kagera Sugar, 08.2016). Local peasants are free to opt into or out of the new mode of production introduced by the company. And beyond low pay and difficult working conditions, their reluctance to sign on with the company also reflects cultural factors. The Missenyi district was previously part of the Haya kingdoms, and people who identify as Haya place a high value on education. Throughout Tanzania, the Haya are generally recognized as one of the country's most highly educated groups (fieldnotes and observations 2016–17). As a result, a significant portion of the local population places a low social value on the employment opportunities offered by Kagera Sugar. The company must therefore recruit staff from other Tanzanian regions – most of those who live on the plantation do not come from nearby communities – and deal with a high turnover rate among its low-skilled workers. Meanwhile, most local workers prefer to live in their home villages, even when this means commuting to the plantation every day (interviews farmers and villagers from nine villages, Kagera region, 2016–17). So, while it is true that villagers are adapting to the new politico-economic conditions, most of those I interviewed are seeking to maintain their independence from the company. Although they appreciate the opportunities offered by Kagera Sugar, they tend to take the jobs it offers only when they need cash to pay school fees or buy farm inputs, or when the harvest is not as good as expected. And as soon as their situation improves, they usually return to working the family farm. They prefer the flexibility and independence offered by small-scale farming, even if that sometimes means barely producing enough to survive. In addition to its cultural value, land serves as a safety net for peasants. The villagers I met with appreciated both the cultural value of having their own land and the security it provided. Few of them were willing to abandon their traditional livelihood in favour of a new mode of production, such as the one proposed by the company. As Murray Li (2011, p. 295) notes, 'In the absence of national welfare provisions, even a tiny patch of land is a crucial safety net'. Indeed, whereas some aspects of Kagera Sugar's operations support Glassman's (2006) argument regarding the semi-proletarianization of the peasantry through capitalist penetration and concomitant processes of primitive accumulation, the company's arrival has only had a marginal effect on how most local peasants support themselves. And as sugar production becomes increasingly mechanized, the impact will further diminish. Villagers are neither actively resisting Kagera Sugar nor passively integrating into its capitalist mode of production as semi-proletarians. Rather, most of them are reacting to developments in a way that fosters their interests. They agree to sell their labour when they have a specific need for cash but return to their traditional occupations once the need has passed.

Yet the arrival of Kagera Sugar has affected local communities in other ways. In the following sections, I explore how the company safeguards its operational profitability, which relies on a regional monopoly and monopsony over sugar, by cultivating clientelistic relations at the national and local level. These activities have led to the emergence of new local patrons who use their positions to enrich themselves, often at the expense of the larger community.

The impact of clientelistic relations on the local agrarian political economy

Tanzania's politics of sugar

Tanzania has a highly regulated sugar market, composed of just four active companies. Due to poor technology and low productivity, the country's producers would likely not survive in a free and open international market. In fact, domestic sugar production has failed to meet internal demand (MAFAP, 2012; 'Agribusiness country diagnostic Tanzania', 2016), and the government periodically issues import permits to select foreign buyers. Tight state control over sugar imports serves not only to protect the domestic sugar industry, but also to make support of local production very politically lucrative (Eriksen,

2018, p. 24). The sugar crisis of 2016 illustrates the highly politicized nature of sugar production in Tanzania. When Magufuli took power in November 2015, he cast himself as the enemy of corruption. Setting out to reform how sugar import permits were issued, he transferred responsibility from the Tanzania Sugar Board to the Prime Minister's Office (interview programme manager, Sugar Board of Tanzania, 10.2016). However, by early 2016, administrative delays had sparked a national sugar crisis, with significant shortages lasting several weeks. As sugar prices peaked, the government's handling of the crisis became a major issue that was closely followed by the national media (e.g. Kamndaya, 2016; Tairo, 2016). The government publicly blamed sugar dealers, who hoarded their reserves to draw maximum benefit from the surge in prices, accusing them of threatening not just the Tanzanian economy but also national security. It is impossible to say if the government deliberately created the shortage for the benefit of its political allies, sugar dealers and importers, or if it was just a matter of incompetence and lack of foresight. Although Magufuli's exact motives remain unclear, his actions would appear to reflect the current state of affairs in Tanzanian politics, characterized by clientelistic dynamics and the close alignment of business and political interests (Cooksey and Kelsall, 2011; Cooksey, 2012; Andreoni, 2017; Eriksen, 2018). Perhaps Magufuli was responding to pressure from the business community and/or his fellow CCM members. Many of those who led the privatization process in the 1990s now owned shares in the country's sugar producers, and a sharp increase in prices certainly would have been to their advantage.

Whatever the case, the government's response to the crisis clearly increased its control over who would receive import permits. By asserting more direct authority over the international sugar trade through the Prime Minister's Office, the president was able to protect the existing oligopoly's dominance over production and distribution, while opening new opportunities for the small number of domestic producers. Ultimately, the entire sugar crisis – which was both caused and resolved by Magufuli's government – was more than an economic issue. It was also a cleverly seized political opportunity. The national media's extensive coverage of the crisis cast Magufuli as an effective populist leader. More importantly, under the guise of fighting corruption, Magufuli was able to assert his authority and take control of the clientelistic networks associated with the importation and distribution of sugar (e.g. see Andreoni, 2017, p. 33). Furthermore, the crisis served to highlight the political importance of sugar. Operating in a tightly regulated market, Tanzanian sugar companies need to leverage their political connections in order to effectively produce, process, and distribute this lucrative commodity. As Eriksen (2018, p. 24) explains, 'Sugar [in Tanzania] is a well-established industry with few players, reliance on a domestic market, and a structural deficit that has created significant rents. Responses to rent-seeking in the sugarcane sector show that even when producers and processors are well organized, criminal practices can continue to hold back a key industry.'

How Kagera Sugar cultivates clientelistic relations and secures political protection

Kagera Sugar is the only domestic producer in Tanzania that enjoys a regional monopoly on sugar production and processing. I argue that this unique advantage reflects the company's commitment to cultivating clientelistic relations at the national level. And although it would be nearly impossible to find conclusive evidence, three significant factors support this argument. First, Kagera Sugar is the only national sugar producer that can still expand horizontally. Unlike its competitors, the company can acquire new lands and enjoys unlimited access to irrigation from the Kagera River – a significant and underutilized water source. Over the medium term, the company is therefore seeking to expand its operations and capture a larger share of the national market (interview chief of operations, Kagera Sugar, 08.2016; Author 2016, interview programme manager Sugar Board of Tanzania, 10.2016). The good relations Kagera Sugar has built with local communities will facilitate this expansion by allowing the company to acquire new land directly from surrounding villages. Land deals negotiated with village leaders are directly formalized by the Ministry of Land, without the involvement or even knowledge of authorities at the district level (interviews Missenyi district official, 08.2016). This reversal of information flows makes the district dependent on the company for information on land acquisitions, whereas most empirical studies of farmland acquisition in Tanzania emphasize the pivotal role played by district officials (see for instance Chapter 5, and Engström, Bélair and Blache, 2018). Clearly, Superdoll's political connections have allowed it to secure preferential treatment from central authorities and the ability to bypass local governance structures. At the local level, my respondents often suggested that the company's lands were owned by individuals other than the official owners, and that Kagera Sugar is connected to a former high-level CCM politician. Although such rumours are difficult to confirm, West and Haug (2017, p. 13) report similar allegations by villagers in their study of Superdoll's Mtibwa Sugar Estate in Kilombero, Tanzania.

Second, whereas Tanzanian sugar companies must compete with each other elsewhere in the country, Kagera Sugar enjoys a regional monopoly on the commodity. During my research, I interviewed three local businessmen, all of whom had been forced to abandon attempts to break into the regional sugar market after encountering political difficulties. Third, Kagera Sugar also enjoys a regional monopsony. Indeed, it is the only Tanzanian sugar company with an outgrower programme that deals with a single outgrower association. By contrast, its counterparts elsewhere in the country, such as the Kilombero Sugar Company, must deal with numerous different outgrower associations. This creates stiff competition and increases administrative and financial costs (e.g. Mmari, 2015). Meanwhile, Kagera Sugar has been able to avoid the drawbacks associated with a more competitive production market, and the company's political connections ensure the failure of any challenges to the established order. For example, in 2014, Missenyi district commissioner (who was an outgrower himself) began to lay the groundwork for a new outgrower association. Not only did his efforts fail, but the former president personally stepped in to transfer him to another district and replace him with a more compliant public servant (fieldnotes and interviews with outgrowers, 2016–17). At the local level, political protection also allows Kagera Sugar to co-opt the leaders of the region's lone outgrower association and the latter's microfinance programme. The company therefore enjoys total control over contract farming in the district, giving it a major financial advantage. Naturally, co-opted local elites are rewarded financially for their compliance. And as the following section explains, such clientelistic dynamics are key to understanding the local impact of the company's contract farming programme. Essentially, by drawing on its political influence at the national level, Kagera Sugar has been able to further protect its interests by establishing a similar clientelistic system at the local level.

The impact of clientelistic relations at the local level

Monopolistic management of contract farming

As part of its efforts to expand production (see above), Kagera Sugar established an outgrower scheme in 2007–8. Buying sugarcane from outgrowers allows the company to maximize production, since its milling capacity currently exceeds its ability to grow sugarcane. The arrangement also provides the local population with an interesting economic opportunity: in the general absence of a market for other crops, the company offers a guaranteed price for sugarcane. Numerous small- and medium-scale farmers in the area have therefore acquired land to produce the crop. However, the system remains highly regulated. In particular, all outgrowers must register with Kaziba, the district's sole outgrower association. In theory, Kaziba is responsible for providing outgrowers with training, improved seeds, fertilizer, assistance with harvesting and transportation services. The association also negotiates the price at which outgrowers sell sugarcane to the company. In 2016, 384 outgrowers were registered with Kaziba. Although they come from different backgrounds, most of them are Haya from the Missenyi district who have developed small-scale sugarcane plantations (one to fifteen hectares) on their own land to supplement their farming revenues. In cases where they acquire additional land, they usually do so through their village leaders (fieldnotes and observations 2016–17). However, some individuals originally from the Kagera region who now live in larger cities (such as Dar es Salaam or Mwanza) have acquired larger parcels of land (fifty hectares and more) for sugarcane plantations. These outgrowers normally have access to capital, as well as political connections in the Kagera region. In recent years, they have been successful in leveraging their political influence at the local and national level, to take advantage of investment opportunities by acquiring substantial amounts of new land. These investors belong to a different social category – what I call wealthy emigrants.[2] In most cases, such medium-scale, elite investors hire local managers to oversee their plantations and business operations, and only occasionally visit the area in person.

Although Kaziba was initially created by farmers to increase their bargaining power with the company, its leaders appear to be increasingly focused on using their positions for personal gain (fieldnotes and observations, 2016–17).

Naturally, this has caused a few problems, including a lack of transparency in negotiations; delays in payment; unfulfilled commitments to provide training and access to inputs, such as improved seeds and fertilizer; transportation issues; rising membership fees; and increased administrative costs. However, not all outgrowers have been equally affected. According to my interviews, those with the biggest plantations and best political connections tend to face fewer transportation issues, payment delays and troubles accessing inputs. Moreover, they usually have better access to capital, allowing them to operate independently of SACCOS, the microfinance agency that has a monopoly on the provision of small loans to outgrowers in the district. By contrast, most small-scale outgrowers must cope with apparent collusion between Kaziba and SACCOS. The association strongly encourages its members to take out high-interest loans from the microfinance agency. However, SACCOS generally forbids them from settling their loans in a single payment, preferring to receive multiple instalments over a longer period. In the words of one outgrower I interviewed,

> When you get a loan with SACCOS, you [have] to pay very high-interest rates and they are blocking you from reimbursing your loan at once when you get the money. They want you to go by installments. SACCOS is even sometimes taking up my money directly from what the company should pay me, without even consulting me. How is it possible? I got a loan once with them, and I will never do it again. I hate SACCOS. I got a loan of TSH 3 million [US$ 2.000] for six months. I had to pay TSH 800,000 [US$ 533] in interest. I paid all at once, but I will never do it again.
>
>   (interview with an outgrower, Missenyi district, 01.2017)

These institutional arrangements have placed many outgrowers in a difficult financial position. Once association fees and loan payments are deducted from their sales, most of them are left with almost nothing. One of my respondents told me that many of them cannot even afford to send their children to school. In short, the realities of contract farming in the region do not fully match the international mainstream narrative (Deininger and Byerlee, 2011) that praises microcredit initiatives and outgrowing schemes for empowering farmers economically. As Vicol (2017, p. 157) notes in his analysis of contract farming in India, outgrowers are not excluded; rather, they are adversely included. This echoes the findings of other recent studies on the difficulties faced by farmers who participate in agricultural schemes (De Schutter, 2011; Oya, 2012; Burnod, Gingembre and Ratsialonana, 2013; West and Haug, 2017). Moreover, SACCOS's monopoly tends to support McMichael's (2013, p. 674) contention that debt relations are increasingly used as disciplining tools.

Likewise, the existing literature shows that the socially differentiated impacts observed in the Kagera region – with larger landowners faring better than smaller ones – reflect similar trends elsewhere. However, my analysis helps to explain the reasons and causes behind such social differentiation. Specifically, clientelistic relations and political protection at the national level in Tanzania have had lasting repercussions on the agrarian political economy at the local level. This has led to the emergence, co-opting, and empowerment of new local elites (i.e. the leaders of Kaziba and SACCOS, as well as wealthy emigrants). Furthermore, these impacts have been felt well beyond contract farming. As the next section demonstrates, the rising demand for land has created new economic incentives for land control. In the Kagera region, this has led district officials to take control of land formalization and use the process to unlawfully dispossess villagers. Despite being illegal, such practices appear to be tolerated because they benefit other actors, namely district officials and wealthy emigrants interested in acquiring the valuable lands at the lower prices. To use the metaphor of the politics of the belly (Bayart, 1989), district officials are allowed to have their share of the cake if they help others eat.

District officials' capture of land formalization processes

This rising demand for land has caused prices to soar, with adverse consequences for villagers. For instance, most small farmers lack formal title to their land and are therefore very vulnerable to dispossession.[3] Instances of local leaders or district officials using their power to strip villagers of their land rights have only increased since leasing village lands to outgrowers has emerged as a lucrative business. Meanwhile, land formalization has become both more complicated and more politicized. Anyone seeking to have their land surveyed and titled must pay district officials, who often misrepresent the legal parameters and costs associated with the process. But the fact remains that most villagers lack the financial resources required to pursue the only real option for protecting their land rights, namely securing title to their land. In Missenyi, district officials have also been very innovative and have subverted land formalization processes to capture the economic benefits arising from land commodification. As already argued in Chapter 4, the district officials responsible for developing VLUPs have manipulated the process to make land available to investors, thereby securing personal gain at the expense of local villagers. Typically, these officials exclude certain parts of a village from the official plan and threaten any village leaders who dare to contest the newly established boundaries. In most cases, the territory cut off from the village is immediately ceded to wealthy emigrants (interviews villagers and villages' leaders, Missenyi district, 2016–17).

Administrative transfer constitutes a second strategy used by district officials to seize control of valuable land. Regulated by the Local Government Acts 1982 and its subsequent amendments,[4] which puts district officials in charge of planning, it involves incorporating village lands into new towns, which fall under the Urban Land Act 2007 rather than the Village Land Act 1999. As part of the process, villagers are required to cede their land rights – in the form of Certificates of Customary Rights of Occupancy (CCROs) – to the state, in exchange for compensation, resettlement or an option to buy land in the newly created town. Not only do villagers lose the right to control what had previously been village lands, they are forced to sell these lands at predetermined rates that are far below market value. The government justifies the process by arguing that it not only streamlines land administration, but also increases land values. However, the value added to the land through administrative transfer is captured by district officials charged with managing the new towns, not the villagers who most often cannot afford to buy back their ancestral land. For example, for reasons that remain unclear, district officials in Missenyi are seeking to transform a village called Bunazi into a town. The village is neither the biggest nor the most populous in the area. However, Bunazi is located near Kagera Sugar, meaning that wealthy emigrants would be interested in acquiring its lands for contract farming. Changing the village's administrative status would therefore provide a way for district officials to benefit from rising property values, by legally dispossessing villagers and transferring the village lands to investors, be they wealthy emigrants or political allies. In fact, the inhabitants of Bunazi believe that district officials had already found buyers for the land before they even initiated the process (interviews villagers Bunazi village, Missenyi district, 2016–17). Overall, administrative transfer reflects the deep-rooted paternalism of the Tanzanian state, which assumes that only central authorities can *properly* manage village lands and that villagers – or 'backward peasants' – need to be guided through the socio-economic development process as villages expand (Ingle, 1970; Constant Martin, 1988; Scott, 1998; Schneider, 2014). Such a means of dispossessing peasants also fits with Akram-Lodhi's argument (2007, p. 1444) that dispossession by accumulation entails two complementary political modes of forcible separation. On the one hand, the dominant classes rely on market mechanisms to appropriate land for themselves. On the other hand, they pursue reforms that restructure the allocation of resources in their favour. Likewise, Peluso and Lund (2011, p. 670) highlight how the dual role of land authorities as both regulators and rent seekers is key to understanding those processes of dispossession.

As mentioned above, control of land formalization has provided district officials with a way of transferring land to wealthy emigrants. The latter also form part of the local political elite, insofar as they frequently have ties to either the regional or district administration of the CCM and therefore enjoy political protection and preferential treatment in the context of land distribution and titling (fieldnotes, interviews and observations 2016–17). Furthermore, wealthy emigrants also benefit from political connections at the national level, where patrons pursue land redistribution as part of their political strategy (Andreoni, 2017; Eriksen, 2018). These political connections at the local and national level provide district officials with not only the authority to proceed with their sometimes illegal or violent land formalization efforts, but also the promise of political protection. Nor are clientelistic relations a new factor in relation to land management in the Kagera district. Shivji (1992, pp. 28–30) notes that, as early as 1992, villagers frequently complained about both the arbitrary distribution of land by the government and their loss of control over rural and village lands. So notwithstanding the market-oriented reforms of the 1990s and the implementation of the Village Land Act 1999, not much has changed in how government officials approach land management. Indeed, Bryceson's assessment of the situation in 1991 remains relevant today:

> Ironically, it is the state itself or its agents, that have become the target of farmers' grievances. State agents, exercising their largely unsupervised discretionary powers, can engage in corrupt practices for the enhancement of their landholdings or commercial interests. On the other hand, the state, both at national and regional levels, acting in the name of 'public interests' can, in the eyes of local farmers, be trampling on their customary rights to land.
>
> (Bryceson, 1991, p. 3, qtd Shivji, 1992, p. 116)

However, not only are administrative processes now being used much more extensively to strip villagers of their land rights in the Missenyi district, but this accelerated process of dispossession is directly associated with the arrival of Kagera Sugar and the company's impact on the regional economy. As discussed in the next section, the politicization of land formalization has affected the local agrarian system by altering social dynamics and production processes, as well as by intensifying existing local dynamics of social differentiation. Furthermore, these changes disproportionately affect the district's most vulnerable populations – migrants, youth and women – making them the silent victims of clientelistic relations.

Migrants are not 'Real' villagers

Numerous factors explain why increasing numbers of foreign and internal migrants have been arriving in the district. To begin with, Kagera Sugar actively recruits migrant labourers to fill its lowest-paying jobs. In recent decades, conflicts in Uganda, Rwanda and Burundi have also forced residents of those countries to seek refuge in the area. Finally, many of those who fled during the Tanzania–Uganda War of 1978–79 subsequently returned to the district, creating complex dynamics of internal migration. Nevertheless, the proportion of migrants remains small. Most villagers identify as Haya, and their families have been present in the region for multiple generations (fieldnotes and observations 2016–17). Meanwhile, migrants often settle on the outskirts of villages, where undeveloped land was still available at the time of their arrival. Some have lived in the area for more than two generations, thereby acquiring customary rights of occupancy on the land they cultivate. However, most migrants never fully integrate into village life and find themselves excluded from local politics based on their origin. As a result, local leaders are less willing to defend their land rights, making them easy targets for district officials seeking to acquire land for wealthy emigrants. As Chapter 7 details, the case of a sub-village near Kagera Sugar is an illustrative example. Following a series of illegal and violent eviction operations in 2008 and 2016, and amid ongoing political intimidation, the population was ultimately removed by force in October 2017. With assistance from the military, district officials even burned the houses of the evicted villagers. Eight politically well-connected wealthy emigrants had already purchased the land and began using it for contract farming almost immediately (interview leaders sub-village, 01.2017).

Women and youths

An acute land shortage means there is often nothing for local youth to inherit. The significance of this issue lies in how it affects the community's relationship to land, which is traditionally passed on from father to son. In short, villagers fear they will not be able to leave anything to their children and see the land shortage as an important cause of youth unemployment. Indeed, local youth have few options when it comes to earning a living. Jobs are available at Kagera Sugar, but as mentioned above, they are not culturally valued. Local young people can also start small businesses. Indeed, many of them have become *boda boda* (motorbike) drivers, although such work is seen as temporary due to the limited possibility of earning a decent livelihood. Finally, outgrowers often hire youth to perform physically demanding work, such as land clearing or weeding. In most cases, the land manager will negotiate payment per task, rather than paying young people an hourly wage. As a result, undervalued tasks tend to be extremely poorly paid. And since these activities constitute casual employment, they come with no job security, equipment or insurance. Nevertheless, the workers I interviewed pointed out that working for an outgrower gives them more flexibility in terms of working hours than a job at Kagera Sugar. Meanwhile, the growing number of young people finding casual employment provides yet another illustration of class differentiation in the area, as wealthy outgrowers belonging to an emerging middle class hire labourers to work their lands. This situation reflects a profound change in the agrarian political economy: Missenyi youth are increasingly losing control over the means of production and relying on casual labour to survive.

Although there is no evidence Kagera Sugar engages in gender discrimination, few women apply to work for the company. Cultural norms greatly restrict women's opportunities for working outside the home. Rather, Tanzanian women are expected to work on their family's land, perform domestic tasks, and manage expenses related to children (fieldnotes and observations 2016–17). However, land scarcity has begun to impact family labour systems. And while men are increasingly unable to earn a living by working their own land, my interviews with married women suggest that the wages these men earn from employers often fail to cover family expenses. Men frequently refuse to disclose their actual earnings to their wives, preferring to maintain as much flexibility as possible in terms of their personal spending (interviews farmers and villagers from nine villages, Kagera region, 2016–17). As a result, women are left to bear the hidden costs of a changing agrarian political economy. Left to their own devices, they must find a way to cultivate the family land and meet the needs of their children. As Glassman (2006, p. 618) notes, women's unpaid social reproductive labour is a key condition for extra-economic accumulation under changing agrarian dynamics.

Conclusion

This chapter has taken a case-study approach to understanding the impact of farmland investments on the local agrarian political economy in one area of Tanzania. I have argued that Kagera Sugar's regional monopoly and monopsony within a projected national market has allowed the company to cultivate clientelistic relations at the national and local level. Furthermore, the structuring impact of these clientelistic relations on actors' interactions is key to understanding the company's impact on the local agrarian system. Clientelistic relations of power allow Kagera Sugar to exert political influence and assert its privileges. This has led to the emergence of many new local patrons who seek personal gain at the expense of community well-being. Indeed, the arrival of Kagera Sugar transformed the local political economy by creating winners and losers at the local level. The biggest winners include district officials, wealthy emigrants and local political elites, as well as the leaders of the district outgrower association and microfinance agency. They have been able to personally profit from the situation by engaging in clientelistic relations that serve the interests of Kagera Sugar, local elites and the central state. For instance, district officials have benefited from land scarcity and the recent surge in land prices by manipulating land formalization in a way that also allows wealthy emigrants and other elites to acquire valuable land for contract farming at very low cost.

Granted, my analysis has shown that, to some extent, the peasantry also benefits from Kagera Sugar's presence. The company provides employment, contributes to local socio-economic development and allows communities to mitigate the risks associated with small-scale agriculture through economic diversification. But not only are these benefits unevenly distributed, they are likely to diminish over time. For example, small outgrowers increasingly find themselves in financial difficulty, while the low-paying jobs and difficult working conditions offered by Kagera Sugar are unlikely to provide a long-term solution to poverty. Moreover, because the investments made by the company tend to reinforce existing dynamics of social differentiation, the area's most vulnerable populations – migrants, youth and women – have emerged as the biggest losers. As their land rights become increasingly insecure, these groups have limited options for earning a livelihood. I therefore conclude that farmland investments tend to consolidate existing dynamics of differentiation at the local level. I also underscore the role played by clientelistic relations in shaping local production models, practices and outcomes by explicitly linking them to clientelistic politics at the national level.

More broadly, these dynamics reflect a more profound agrarian transformation underway in rural Tanzania. As many scholars have pointed out, a new middle class is emerging (Cooksey, 2012; Sulle, 2017; Bluwstein et al., 2018; Jayne et al., 2019). However, it is important to recognize that changes in the local agrarian political economy are multicausal. Indeed, clientelistic relations intersect with other factors such as the implementation of the global development agenda on land formalization and privatization, as well as the push for commercial agricultural models. Furthermore, clientelistic relations are embedded within larger historical and socio-economic dynamics related to family strategies, gender inequality, population growth and decreasing land fertility.

Village politics, or a micro political arena. Negotiating inclusion by exclusion, or how to secure 'eating' from farmland investments

This chapter focuses on the impacts of land investments at the village level, by analysing and comparing the sequence of two land conflicts that have resulted from the increased presence of investors in a specific village, Village X, located in Kagera region. As documented in Chapter 6, I discovered that the local impacts associated with the arrival of Kagera Sugar were far more extensive than I first expected. Besides attracting many new Tanzanian investors in the district, it transformed the local political economy in several ways. Land prices have peaked in surrounding villages because of increased land scarcity in the district, the company's contract farming programme has induced class differentiation dynamics, and district officials have found innovative ways of capturing land formalization processes to free land for investors and political friends. This, in turn, has fostered local land conflicts. Moreover, the reactions of local leaders to these investors varied: their involvement in land conflicts differed not only from one village to the next, but also within the same village. For instance, Village X is involved in two important land conflicts related to

An earlier version of this chapter has been published in the *Canadian Journal of African Studies* in 2020. See: Bélair, J. (2020) 'Negotiating inclusion by exclusion, or how to secure "eating" from farmland investments in Tanzania', *Canadian Journal of African Studies / Revue canadienne des études africaines*, 0(0), pp. 1–20. doi:10.1080/00083968.2020.1795895 © 2020, Taylor & Francis Ltd, 'Reprinted with permission'.

the arrival of these new investors. Interestingly, village leaders have defended their villagers' land rights in the first land conflict, but chose to partner with political elites and Tanzanian investors to foster their material interests at the expense of a sub-set of villagers in the other. In addition to showing that local reactions cannot be assumed to be constant in time and space, these observations raise two questions: Why do local leaders address local land conflicts with different strategies? And, more specifically, why did leaders mobilize around autochthony in one case but not in the other?

To answer these questions, three key elements constituting the S of the local CAS should be considered. The first is the role played by institutions and historical legacies in structuring the range of possibilities for local reactions. This argument relates to Boone's contention that national rural land institutions determine 'patterned variations in the structure and political character of land-related competition and conflict' (Boone, 2014, p. 3). Accordingly, the role played by the central state in Tanzania is assumed to be direct both in land allocation and in solving land conflictual dynamics, because of the country's national statist land tenure regime (Boone and Nyeme, 2015, p. 70). Yet, although considering the Tanzanian formal and centralized structure for land attribution and conflict management is important, such a perspective downplays the role informal institutions play in shaping local dynamics of power which are often played out outside formal institutions (Gray, 2018, p. 22). In addition, this overestimates the success of centralization processes. As several scholars have pointed out, centralization has remained at best partial in Tanzania, especially at the local level (Andreoni, 2017; Kelsall, 2018). For instance, Boone's argument overlooks the impacts of clientelistic relationships on conflict management. However, and second, this chapter shows that clientelistic relations of power are an important component of the local CAS, and considering their impact helps understanding why leaders have used different strategies in these two conflicts.

The third structuring element is the politics of belonging given their influence on local claims to land and in determining who has the legitimacy to make them. Recent works have emphasized how the instrumentalization of autochthony is key to understanding land conflicts and the local impacts of land investments (Badiey, 2013; Bromwich, 2017; Wittig, 2017). As scholars have documented in Africa and elsewhere, the politics of belonging induce local dynamics of social differentiation that actors may use to foster their interests (Bayart, Geschiere and Nyamnjoh, 2001; Geschiere and Jackson, 2006; Dunn, 2009; Côté and Mitchell, 2017). Thus, considering local leaders' claims to being 'sons of the soil' helps us to understand how they negotiate their position of power within the local CAS and with actors at other levels of governance. For example, Mkodzongi (2016) shows that local chiefs' claim to ancestral autochthony has been crucial in legitimizing their political authority in the context of new investments. In Ghana, both Anaafo and Guba (2017) and Ubink (2008) contend that local authorities are taking advantage of their proclaimed autochthonous status to partner with the state and investors to dispossess and alienate the poorest and most marginalized farmers. However, for the specific case of Tanzania, the literature generally assumes that this variable should not play a role. Autochthony is depicted as being not politically salient in land conflicts because of historical legacies: Nyerere's *ujamaa* policy led to the resettlement of about five million rural Tanzanians during the 1970s, thereby deeply restructuring relations to land and making autochthony claims irrelevant (Hyden, 1980; Lorgen, 2000; Miguel, 2004; Malipula, 2014; Boone and Nyeme, 2015). Yet further analysis demonstrates that such arguments might mislead by downplaying the instrumentalization of ethnic identity and its political saliency in Tanzania.[1] As argued here, documenting how actors leverage politics of belonging to legitimize land claims and dispossession is crucial to understand the trajectories of these two conflicts. Indeed, to explain why the studied cases display very different patterns in the strategies used by the local leaders, we need looking at actors' social action and at how it interplays with the S, making the distribution of power much more contingent than generally acknowledged.

The chapter is divided as follows. After presenting the case study, it examines how, in these two land conflicts, the local CASs have shaped the local distribution of power and conflictual interactions between villagers, state officials and investors. Leaders' strategy in the second conflict differs from the first because they hold enough power to secure their inclusion in local clientelistic networks by rendering politically salient the autochthonous status to exclude a sub-set of villagers. My analysis emphasizes that actors' power holding is contingent in time and space, and insists on how formal and informal institutions are both constraining and enabling actors' agency. It contributes to an emerging scholarship that links the global land rush and land conflicts (Dell'Angelo et al., 2017) by empirically documenting the indirect and complex processes through which new investments made by Tanzanian investors lead to land conflicts. It also challenges the dominant narrative of Tanzania as a harmonious country in which ethnicity is not politically salient by showing that Tanzanian local actors have instrumentalized identity to produce political discrimination. In addition, it provides a counter-narrative to overly optimistic narratives of contract-farming schemes (e.g. Brüntrup et al., 2018) showing how they may indirectly trigger local political struggles that foster land conflicts, land dispossession and social marginalization. Finally, it contributes to our understanding of how the national Tanzanian political settlement (Andreoni, 2017; Kelsall, 2018) translates at the local level, something that has been called for (Behuria, Buur and Gray, 2017) but is still understudied.

Village X in Kagera region: The case study

Village X has a population of approximately 9,000 and is located in the north of Tanzania, west of Lake Victoria, south of Uganda. Even though the region has reliable high rainfalls, soils are of mixed fertility, so land scarcity has long been an important problem in the region (Reining, 1962, p. 72). Village X existed before the colonization of Tanzania and was originally part of the Haya Kingdoms. When Germans arrived in the region, it was inhabited by Haya people and divided into nine different kingdoms. Political power was centralized and social life highly hierarchized and regulated. Local kings in Kagera region remained in power until the Independence of Tanzania in 1961 (Reining, 1962; Carlson, 1993). Historically, Haya land was mostly allocated through inheritance on an individual basis. As documented by Reining (1962, pp. 62–4), in the Haya traditional system, about 66 per cent of land '[was] reallocated through heritance or pre-heritance between landowners and their heirs (men and sons)'. Familial clans were thus especially important in land management (Maruo, 2002).[2] At Independence, President Julius Nyerere dismantled Haya kingdoms: administrative powers were abolished, and the villages' administrative apparatus re-organized with the *ujamaa* policy.

Indeed, nowadays, village administration in Tanzania is responsible for managing village land. According to the 1999 Village Land Act, village land refers to land which is collectively owned by residents of a given village and is vested in the village council (VC) which is appointed by the village assembly (VA). According to the law, the VC is not allowed to allocate land without prior approval of the VA. The VA, which includes all adult village residents, meets every three months to discuss village issues and endorse village leaders' decisions. This structure should theoretically ensure direct accountability of leaders to villagers. In addition, a village executive officer (VEO), a non-elected employee of the state, is named by the district executive director (DED) in each village and assumes diverse administrative functions, including formal allocation of land and issuing land titles. Yet, because of the nomination process, VEOs are not directly accountable to villagers: they report to the district administration. Moreover, in Tanzania, there is a blurring of lines between political and administrative functions of state employees since Independence (Tordoff, 1965). In practice then, non-elected employees of the state, even though they have official non-political administrative functions, are accountable to their administrative superiors and to their politically nominated hierarchical superiors. VEOs are thus in practice informally subordinated and accountable to the district commissioner (DC). The DC in Tanzania is politically nominated, directly appointed by the president. As already mentioned, they are the highest authority at the district level and exert a considerable influence on district management. In addition, it is worth noting that some VEOs and village leaders are seeking to take advantage of their administrative powers for personal benefit (e.g. Fitzgerald, 2017, pp. 25–6).

In Village X, in addition to population growth and decreasing soil fertility, land scarcity has been exacerbated in the last fifteen years (Theodory, 2017, p. 276). Indeed, Village X is now surrounded by investment projects. On one side, there is the Kagera Sugar plantation and its sugar factory, covering about 25,000 hectares. As I discuss in Chapter 6, Kagera Sugar has put in place a contract farming scheme, which has attracted numerous small- and medium-scale Tanzanian investors who have also acquired land from surrounding villages for sugarcane production. On the other side, a national parastatal agency, the National Ranching Company (Narco), has rights on 60,000 hectares of land. In 2002, Narco started the process of subdividing and leasing this land to investors engaged in the livestock business. Therefore, Village X is now sharing boundaries with several Narco investors, whose presence accentuates pressure on vital resources such as grazing areas for cattle and access to water. This multiplication of investors has reinforced the importance of formalizing land boundaries,[3] but this process has turned out to be highly contentious. Village X received its VLUP and village land title in 2015 from district officials. However, village leaders consider that the officially recognized village boundaries were flawed, causing village land dispossession. The confusion stems from the fact that the land claimed by both Narco and Kagera Sugar was left abandoned for several decades, and villagers have thus been using it. According to Tanzanian law, if villagers have been occupying and using land for twelve years or more, this land should become village land (The Village Land Act 1999, 44). Yet it is unclear whether the law will be enforced and whether the contentious land belongs to Village X or not. Consequently, village boundaries have remained contested to this day in Village X, leading to land conflicts between villagers and those investors.

Village X against Missenyi Ranch: Conflict 1

The conflict between Missenyi Ranch and Village X started around 2006 and has been ongoing for several years. Contentious land boundaries are its root cause. Village X claims that all land up to River Y belongs to them, while Narco asserts that it has owned this land since 1969. Narco is a parastatal organization under the Ministry of Agriculture, which is registered under the Company Act of Tanzania. The agency was created in 1967 with the enactment of the *ujamaa* policy. The land that was previously assigned to the groundnut scheme put in place by British colonial authorities was then reattributed to Narco. Thus, Narco inherited rights of occupancy on about 600,000 hectares of land throughout the whole country (interviews with Narco officials, 2016–17). Narco is profit-oriented: its mission is to commercialize land under its control. Usually, Narco proceeds through joint ventures with commercial livestock investors. In 2002, a central cabinet directive obliged Narco to subdivide some parts of its ranches into blocks and to sublease them to Tanzanian investors. The rationale underlying this change was to give land access to small- and medium-scale Tanzanian investors to foster livestock production. In addition to leasing its land at low cost, Narco was also tasked with overseeing these new commercial ventures by providing training and sharing its expertise (interviews with Narco officials, 2016–17). This directive led Narco to lease more than half of its land – about 370,000 out of 600,000 hectares. In Missenyi District where Village X is located, Narco's land – about 60,000 hectares – was divided into twenty-two blocks that were subsequently leased to different Tanzanian investors. These blocks now make up what is known locally as the Missenyi Ranch.

Bottling up the conflict at the district level

As stated, the issue is about land boundaries. The leaders of Village X argue that five blocks of Missenyi Ranch are located on their village land. Therefore, the village's complaint is that, first, it should have been consulted before being dispossessed of its land, and second, it should have been compensated for its loss. This contested land has vital importance for villagers, especially in the current context of acute land scarcity. Most of them combine animal husbandry and farming activities. Access to water and pasture in this context is crucial. These five Narco investors deprived the village of access to an important area that had been commonly and freely used by herders for grazing. In addition, the location of these investors' blocks restrains villagers' access to water (river Y), which is very problematic during the dry season because local herders lack alternative options for watering animals. Consequently, relations between villagers and investors' employees became tense and highly conflictual. This led to an increase of violence between them: several accounts of beatings and killings have been reported in the area. The village leadership tried to solve the conflict at first directly with the concerned investors. For instance, the village chairman frequently visited the blocks in 2008–9 to voice villagers' concerns and attempt to defend their rights by speaking with investors' representatives. This process was unsuccessful because investors kept refusing to acknowledge the village's authority on the contested land. Furthermore, the village chairman's personal involvement in the conflict triggered an escalation of violence: people associated with these investors ambushed and violently attacked him in retaliation for his activism (interviews with the local leaders of Village X,

2016–17). This failure to solve the conflict through local negotiations forced the village leaders to start official procedures of conflict solving.

When such a land conflict occurs in Tanzania, if local resolution of the conflict is unsuccessful, as it was in this case, villages are required to follow a highly hierarchical process. First, they should address their grievances to district authorities. If the district cannot solve the conflict, it goes to regional authorities. Only if regional authorities are incapable of finding a solution is the conflict filed within the national conflict registry and becomes the responsibility of the Ministry of Land. In practice, very few land conflicts in Tanzania reach the ultimate central level during the resolution process: most of them are resolved at lower administrative levels (interview with Ministry of Land, 09.2016). This centralized structure for solving land conflicts creates an opportunity for local actors to have a voice at the national level, as argued by Boone (2014), but this outcome is only possible if all actors involved agree to recognize the conflict, and to move it up the chain of command. Concomitantly, it also means that such conflicts can get stuck at a certain level, contained by designated authorities. This is initially what happened with this conflict: district authorities did not acknowledge it, and consequently, the conflict remained bottled up at the district level for about ten years. Concretely, Village X leaders raised their issues with Missenyi Ranch's investors several times at the district level. District officials asked them to prove that investors were illegally using village land to graze their animals. The village leaders did try to build their case: when investors' cows were grazing on the contested land, they called district officials and asked them to come witness the problem. Yet every time, when district officials arrived, the investors and their cows had disappeared from the contested pasture. Therefore, the district concluded that leaders were mistaken, and that investors were not guilty of any wrongdoing (interviews with Missenyi District officials, 2016–17; interview with the local leaders of Village X, 2017).

However, from the village leaders' angle, it was clear that someone, working at the district level, or even a villager, was colluding with these investors and informing them of the district's upcoming visits, thereby allowing investors to hide before the arrival of officials. Several villagers also believe that investors were bribing district officials to turn a blind eye to the issue. This hide-and-seek game went on for some months. Seeing that the conflict resolution was not progressing, the leaders tried to raise the issue directly with the regional office. However, they were denied the right to file a complaint because the district had refused to acknowledge the conflict. They also informed their CCM Member of Parliament (MP) of the problem, but did not obtain any significant support until very recently (interview with the local leaders of Village X, 01.2017).

How an MP can change a conflict trajectory

The prevailing local perception is that MPs rarely get involved in village issues unless they have an incentive to do so (fieldnotes and observations, 2016–17). Usually, incentives are political, because of pressures from top officials or concerns for re-election,[4] but they also can be of an economic nature, especially when influential members of the Tanzanian business community who have interests at stake are urging action. As this villager states about the role of the MP in this conflict (with Missenyi Ranch):

> When we raise issues [i.e., conflict] at meetings, leaders promise but nothing is ever really done. They provide no solution. Our leaders are facing important challenges with Missenyi Ranch. For me, the central government [probably referring to Narco, as a government agency] has sold us. It is hard to solve since people involved [investors and MPs] are never around. It is always only their representatives. Our leaders have failed but I don't blame them. The problem is our MP who does nothing.
> (Interview with farmer, Missenyi District, 01.2017)

Thus, the conflict was stuck at the district level until 2016, until the somewhat unexpected intervention of the MP. Village X is part of Nkenge Constituency,[5] which belongs firmly to the CCM. Its MP was then Diodorus Buberwa Kamala (CCM). Kamala was an influential member of the CCM and was also Nkenge MP from 2000 to 2010. However, he was ousted from the CCM, failing to secure its parliamentary nomination from the Party in Nkenge Constituency for the 2010 elections (Mande, 2010; *The Economist, Intelligence Unit*, 2010). The exact nature of the issue that Kamala had with the CCM's leading faction at that time, and whether this resulted from a change of the leading faction within the CCM, is unclear, but apparently Kamala found himself on the wrong side.[6] He then held several positions abroad. When Kamala finished his international mandate, he came back to Kagera region and was the CCM candidate in Nkenge Constituency for the 2015 elections. It is unclear how Kamala got back into CCM's good graces, but since 2015, he has realigned himself with the dominant faction of the party. Kamala's political campaign was based on his promise to bring development and changes for Nkenge residents. For instance, he promised to help solve the many land conflicts, ensure access to health services, and oversee the unfinished development of important roads for commercial activities (Elias, 2015). He won the 2015 election ('Tanzania Parliamentary Results', 2015).

Since the 2015 election, Kamala has taken this land conflict to the central level, thereby significantly altering its trajectory. Kamala's involvement triggered the interest of several high-ranking officials from different ministries – the Ministry of Livestock, the Prime Minister's Office, and the Ministry of Land, among others – whose officials visited the village in January 2017. They called a meeting with villagers and Missenyi Ranch's investors, stating that the land of these contentious blocks was unlawfully occupied and should be given back to Village X. The meeting was tumultuous as investors contested this decision, but in the end, they complied and agreed to give back the land to Village X. Since this meeting, the resolution process has started and involves a multiplicity of actors from different governance levels, including central, regional, district and local, in addition to Narco and its associated investors. Although the outcome of this resolution process is uncertain,[7] villagers are now hopeful: their grievances have been heard, and they believe that central authorities are committed to finding a solution. Moreover, investors have already given back some of the contentious Missenyi Ranch's blocks to villagers. This effectively means that investors can no longer block access to the river or graze their cattle on these blocks that are now village land as they did before with the protection of the district.

In sum, external contingent events created this specific conflict, including a situation of acute scarcity of land fostered by increased investors' interest, and the 2002 policy that forced Narco to sublease its land to Tanzanian investors. The sequence of events shows that the institutional makeup influenced the distribution of power and how actors could negotiate land issues. At first, district officials and Narco investors had the upper hand because of their position within this local CAS. Local leaders' powers were greatly limited because of the district's alleged tendency to collude with those investors, and its denial of the conflict which empowered investors vis-à-vis local leaders. Therefore, institutional constraints structured the way the situation unfolded regarding the official and hierarchical process of solving land conflicts. How the formal institutional structure of land management intersects with the clientelistic relations of power at the local level is well illustrated here by the pivotal role that was played by district officials. District officials hold power in land matters and conflicts because of their institutional role as land planning and local investment authorities. This dual role played by district authorities (both regulators and rent seekers) is also partly attributable to the central Tanzanian political settlement, which influences the distribution of power at the local level. As noted by Andreoni (2017) and Eriksen (2018, p. 30), the broad distribution of rents is a strategy to ensure CCM permanence. Close, institutionalized and clientelistic relationships between the private sector and the state are thus not only observed at the central level but also consolidated at the district level to create new rents and ensure the transfer of resources.

Yet the evolution of the conflict shows that this local CAS structuring actors' interactions is contingent and dynamic. The MP's involvement led to a significant restructuring of the power play between actors in this specific conflict. My understanding is that these local investors were illegally using village land and bribing district officials to turn a blind eye and protect them. District officials also played a role in preventing local leaders from informing higher authorities of the conflict, and of their grievances. Without the intervention of the MP, it is very likely that this land conflict would have remained unknown at regional and central levels, and that investors would have continued to use the contentious blocks with the complicity of district authorities. Therefore, it is only with the involvement of the MP that these investors were caught. As already stated, clientelistic relations of power at lower administrative levels are usually tolerated and 'suffer from a lack of control' (Cooksey and Kelsall, 2011) unless there is a central political interest to get involved, as was the case here with the MP's concern for re-election. Again, this links back to the central political settlement as the current president, Magufuli, who was ruling with a vulnerable authoritarian coalition, must support people loyal to him (Eriksen, 2018, p. 30). Here, the centralized structure for conflict management was used to discipline district authorities and to protect Kamala's political career. To avoid problems, district officials played innocent, as if they were not aware. In addition, they lost their structural power to contain the conflict. As a result, Narco investors lost their strategic positioning by losing district officials' support, and therefore found themselves lacking power. They were blamed and disciplined by central authorities and forced to give back some blocks of land to villagers. Local leaders, for their part, were significantly empowered since they gained a voice and support from the central level. It was crucial to defending their fellow villagers in this land conflict with a parastatal agency. Preventing land dispossession also strengthened their political legitimacy in the village.

As the next section demonstrates, however, land conflicts, even if they occur in the same village, do not necessarily unfold similarly. While this second conflict also affected villagers of Village X, its trajectory differs from that of the previous conflict. In this case, village leaders have chosen not to involve central authorities, and to partner instead with district officials and investors. Rather than defending their fellow villagers' land rights, the leaders discriminated against them. This turn of events is explained by the distribution of power in the local CAS structuring this specific conflict. Because the conflict was on land belonging to a sub-village of Village X, village leaders' role as village land planning authorities empowered them. In addition, the villagers affected by this conflict were Tanzanian migrants: excluding them did not endanger the leaders' local political legitimacy. Finally, fostering social differentiation and producing political exclusion allowed the village leaders to secure their inclusion in those clientelistic relations associated with the investment game.

Instrumentalizing belonging to discredit villagers' property claims: Conflict 2

As mentioned earlier and in Chapter 6, the arrival of Kagera Sugar in the region has induced a rising demand for land, which was already a scarce resource. Since the land demarcation process is contentious, and boundaries are not always consensual, new land conflicts have emerged between some wealthy emigrants (see

Chapter 6, p. 91) and villages located near the company. The next section examines such land conflicts by focusing on Matawa, a sub-village of Village X (Matawa is a fictive name). Matawa's location makes its land very attractive for outgrowers interested in selling sugarcane to Kagera Sugar. It is fertile and located near the company, which allows outgrowers to decrease their operating costs because they can use the company's resources for harvesting and transporting sugarcane. Few surrounding sub-villages have this comparative advantage.

Newcomers or allochthones are not 'real' villagers

As previously stated, Village X was historically part of the Haya kingdoms. Consequently, most villagers identify themselves as Haya. Even though most of the villagers in Village X were originally born and raised in the village, a small proportion come from other regions. Although many of these newcomers have been living in Matawa for over three generations, they have never been fully integrated into village politics. Interviews conducted with these villagers reveal important dynamics of social differentiation to exclude villagers based on their origin. An elder originally from Kigoma, of the Muha ethnic group, who has been living in the village for nine years, illustrates the problem during village meetings: 'When I go to meetings, I may not voice my opinions about the village issues. They [village leaders] told us [newcomers] to shut up because these issues do not concern us. We are [forever] foreigners' (interviews with farmers in Missenyi District, 2017). For Matawa, this discrimination is politically significant because most villagers are Tanzanians coming from other regions. Yet, as many Matawa villagers have mentioned, their allochthonous status was not an issue regarding their claims to Village X land when they settled down in the region, some thirty years ago. Village X leaders welcomed them, and gave them parcels of land. Matawa sub-village was then officially acknowledged as part of Village X, and Matawa villagers were duly fulfilling their socio-political obligations although they were sidelined at village meetings.

Recently, however, because this land has increased in value with the arrival of Kagera Sugar in the region, the village leaders have changed their attitude towards Matawa villagers. Many interviewees have highlighted this issue: Village X leaders no longer recognize the existence of the Matawa sub-village, except for the collection of development fees. In the words of one of my informants: 'When they [village leaders] are asked if some people live in the area, they say no, it is only a bush with wild animals'. Another informant expresses how this unexpected rejection from their leaders remains puzzling for Matawa villagers: 'We don't understand why these leaders are mistreating us. Once they got our votes, they forgot about us and even say that we don't exist' (interviews with farmers in Missenyi District, 2017). Politically, the perpetual newcomer status of Matawa villagers explains why they are discriminated against regarding their land rights. Institutionally, as also observed by Greco (2017, p. 175), it is because of the overlap between formal and informal practices of land allocation and distribution that Matawa villagers found themselves in such a vulnerable position. This means that we should not overstate the impacts produced by the *ujamaa* policy on Haya land: in most villages, it led to an overlap between the traditional and the official system of local governance, meaning that although a new administrative apparatus was created and imposed *de jure* at Independence, land remained *de facto* informally managed by familial clans and allocated through inheritance in Kagera region. To give a concrete example of this overlap, in this specific village, the chairman allocates parcels of land to landless villagers, or widows. In exchange, they pay him a tribute every year, depending on their harvest (interviews and fieldnotes, 2016–17). This departs from the official administrative system for village land allocation and creates a relation of political dependency that echoes the pre-colonial *nyarubanja* system (see Note 2, p. 104).

The existence of this overlap demonstrates that the claims regarding the elimination of the traditional governance systems prevailing in Haya land by Nyerere's regime are overstated. As documented by Maruo (2002), implementing the *ujamaa* policy in Haya villages led to few consequential changes. Since Haya were already settled and politically organized in densely populated settlements, regional land commissioners simply renamed existing villages rather than creating new ones. This is not specific to Haya region, and scholars have documented these uneven effects of villagization throughout Tanzania (Cliffe, 1975; Schneider, 2014). For instance, similar dynamics were observed in areas where political power was already centralized, such as the Kilimanjaro and Arusha regions, in which holders of power in precolonial times continued to assert, albeit informally, some form of authority over their communities (Zecki, 1979; Gray, 2018). Therefore, in this case, allochthones' capacity to negotiate with other actors is heavily constrained by historical and institutional legacies, which predetermined the prevailing structural inequalities that explain why distribution of power is unequal among actors within this local CAS. In fact, accounts overwhelmingly suggested that Matawa land is currently being sold to wealthy emigrants by district officials, sometimes in collusion with the VEO of Village X, and possibly with some of its leaders. Apparently, eight politically well-connected wealthy emigrants have already bought parcels of Matawa land and are waiting for the villagers to vacate the area to start production. Because their land rights and even their presence in this location are no longer acknowledged by Village X leaders, Matawa villagers are very vulnerable to illegal political pressures. District officials often resort to violence and intimidation to force villagers to leave the area, and they are normally backed up by the military during these illegal operations. Recently, two significant evictions took place in Matawa, in 2008 and 2016. These dynamics are hidden and politically very contentious. I had to be very careful while investigating this case because Village X leadership, district and military officials were convincingly threatening Matawa villagers. Some even told me that they feared for their lives if they spoke about what was happening. I was myself intimidated several times by district officials, and detained once to verify my research permit and my whereabouts.

Eviction and politics of intimidation: 'Government is like a machete: both sides cut'

In 2008, allochthones were forcefully evicted through an intervention coordinated by the DC in collaboration with the military. This led to an unlawful change of the boundaries of Matawa sub-village, which caused a loss of village land. Subsequently, several investors started production on the vacated area. It created a climate of fear: villagers who had the possibility to move out did. After 2008, the only villagers remaining in Matawa were those lacking such an option, often because they had moved from far away or had no family living nearby (fieldnotes and interviews, 2016–17). More recently, in July 2016, a second operation took place. Again, it was orchestrated by the DC in collaboration with military officials. No one was displaced, but several people were arrested for various reasons. The intervention is locally remembered for its violent character since the army even used tear gas – *mabomu ya machozi* – against unarmed villagers. Most of those who were arrested were fined and later freed (fieldnotes and interviews, 2016–17). In addition to these two major events, Matawa villagers reported that intimidation operations have been common during the whole period. The DC generally comes at night with soldiers to intimidate villagers and tell them they are unlawfully living on this land.

District and military officials use two rationales to justify their actions. Either they claim that this sub-village hides illegal migrants – non-Tanzanians – and they should be arrested and deported, or they would say that Matawa land is part of reserved land for protected forests, and therefore illegally occupied by villagers. In the local context, these arguments failed to convince since there are only two forest reserves registered in the district, and Matawa is not part of either. In addition, most villagers are Tanzanian migrants or newcomers, not illegal migrants (interviews with villagers in Missenyi District, 2016–17). Yet, as so-called migrants or allochthones or newcomers, villagers from this sub-village are disempowered *vis-à-vis* these authorities and have been complying, trying to avoid problems. Matawa villagers fear district and military officials even though they suspect that such harassment is illegal. They lack political power and information to defend their rights. Moreover, to understand their reactions, one should consider the political history of Tanzania, and how people still perceive government authorities as providers but also as the ultimate decision-makers. As a woman states eloquently: '*Serikali ni serikali* [government is the government]. If the government tells you that you must go, you should go. Government is like a machete: both sides cut' (interview with a farmer in Matawa sub-village, 02.2017). In this context, since the district represents the central government, it is hard for vulnerable villagers to contest its authority.

To understand this local conflict and its specific trajectory, it is crucial to consider how local leaders have instrumentalized and rendered autochthonous identity politically salient to redefine their authority towards other actors. Although the conflict was structured by the same contingencies as the previous one, its internal power dynamics differ substantially. Village leaders are powerful players here since they are land management authorities at the village level and their claim to autochthony gave them political capital. They use it to partner with investors, district and military officials, and to benefit from the rising value of Matawa land. Concretely, by excluding Matawa villagers and denying their claims to the land they have been lawfully occupying for several years, they are not only fostering existing socio-political differentiation but also instrumentalizing it for material benefit. Their instrumentalization of the autochthonous norm redefines their political interactions with other actors. While district officials' inaction and collusion with investors were the leaders' objects of grievance in the first conflict, they have developed a relatively complicit relationship with them in this second conflict. Since they are the higher local authorities over all Village X land, including Matawa, their agreement to lease this land allows the district to cover up the illegality of these transactions because it can claim that the village has agreed. Therefore, leaders' position towards Matawa villagers empowers them towards other actors. It permits them to be part of the land dispossession process without fearing political costs and provides a new opportunity to materially benefit from this increased interest in Matawa land from powerful wealthy emigrants. In sum, they managed to acquire sufficient power to be part of this lucrative game, and they use it.

The institutional structure is also especially relevant. It is because of historical and institutional legacies that these leaders have the possibility to draw upon and make the autochthonous norm politically salient. It would not necessarily have been possible, for instance, in other Tanzanian regions, when districts are relatively new and have been only recently populated: there, local communities cannot claim ancestral rights to their land. This also explains why allochthones are structurally excluded from this power game. As already mentioned, actors' capacity to negotiate depends on how much power they hold within a given institutional setting. Although everyone has this ability to negotiate social structure, pre-existing structural inequalities affect actors' possibilities to exert their agency in this local CAS. As I showed with this second conflict, allochthones' power is very constrained. Indeed, Matawa villagers found themselves in an unbearable situation since they are institutionally and politically excluded: their land and even their human rights are continuously denied. They occupy a subordinated position in Village X because of their political status. Their situation remains contained at the very local level, with few prospects of getting visibility at higher levels.

As a matter of fact, there is no official record of even the existence of Matawa sub-village. Furthermore, as of November 2017, the sub-village does not exist anymore. A last eviction operation took place in early November. All remaining villagers were forcefully displaced, and their houses were burned down by military and district officials. The disappearance of Matawa sub-village was witnessed by the author's informants and research assistants. With this last violent eviction, all proof of authorities' wrongdoings was effectively obliterated.

What is particularly interesting about this second land conflict is that it illustrates the contingent temporality of such political discrimination. It is when local leaders have both interest and capacity that they instrumentalize the politics of belonging to secure their inclusion in investment dynamics. The process is thus more dynamic in time and space than what an institutional perspective would suggest. Local leaders rendered the autochthonous norm politically salient at a specific point in time because contingencies (arrival and interest of new investors) made it attractive to do so. Autochthony had not been politically salient regarding land rights in this specific village. Autochthony is not necessarily politically salient in neighbouring villages. Autochthony is therefore a structuring and exclusionary norm, the effects of which are uneven in time and space and depend on which actors are power holders and on their chosen strategy of action.

Conclusion

To conclude, this chapter documented how the arrival of new investors in a Tanzanian village has fostered local land conflicts. It sought to explain why local leaders defended their fellow villagers in one land conflict, but discriminated against them in the other. I argued that unpacking the local CASs of these two conflicts is analytically fruitful to uncover actors' interactions that have shaped the differentiated trajectories of these two conflicts. I showed that the S structures local power relations but may also be instrumentalized by actors to restructure them. In addition, the S, albeit informal and overlapping with the post-colonial administrative one, plays a role in predetermining which actors can negotiate their power position in a given setting. I also drew attention to how local leaders' actions may contribute to identity building when they are instrumentalizing the social structure to foster their material interests. That was the case in this village with the new political saliency of the autochthonous status. It elucidated why the leaders chose in the second conflict to discredit affected villagers' property claims to secure their inclusion in new investment dynamics, and why those villagers remained powerless in the face of these predatory practices. This is a significant finding for the Tanzanian case. To my knowledge, although frequently studied in other African countries, this is one of the few contributions documenting how a sub-set of local actors instrumentalized the autochthonous norm to produce political discrimination regarding local land rights in Tanzania.

Finally, this chapter showed that indirect impacts provoked by new farmland investments in developing countries may be more significant for local communities than the direct ones. For example, in the second conflict, Kagera Sugar has not been directly causing local conflictual dynamics; however, the arrival of the investor has significantly transformed the local political economy. Thus, new investments and associated contract-farming schemes have extensive indirect consequences for the local political economy (i.e. creating opportunities for rent-seeking and fostering political struggles and local land conflicts) that we need to ponder when evaluating their socio-economic outcomes.

8

Concluding remarks

To conclude, this land rush has induced exclusion dynamics and several local issues in Tanzania. As this book showed, few investments are operational, and most of them fail to deliver on their promises. Processes of land acquisitions are plagued with issues. Consultations and compensation of affected communities are almost always problematic. The success of land formalization programmes in securing peasants' land rights is questionable. Investments' monitoring and evaluation beyond acquisition processes are also predominantly deficient. Local grievances are further aggravated when state authorities keep on defending unproductive or absent investors, at the expense of the community who has been dispossessed. Political collusion is also an important problem. State officials, investors and elites, and even sometimes local leaders, use their authority to interfere in farmland acquisition and land formalization processes because they want to secure their participation in the investment game.

This book sought not only to document the local impacts of this global land rush in Tanzania, but also to foster our understanding of why we witness such outcomes. It focused on the transformations of the political economy that are induced by the arrival of new investors, and on how political struggles over land, capital and authority unfold in Tanzania. It argued that unpacking the political interplays associated with new farmland investments is key to understand what is going on, who is benefiting, who is losing and why it is unfolding this way. My analysis relied on CAS, an analytical tool that significantly helped me to unpack and study actors' interactions associated with the land rush in Tanzania. From a theoretical standpoint, this book argued that new farmland investments should be analysed as contingencies, that are both exogenous and endogenous disruptions to the studied systems of political interactions.

Contingencies open new opportunities for actors to exert their agency, and through their actions, to renegotiate the structural components of CAS. We need documenting empirically these negotiation processes because CASs are context-dependent, and should be unpacked in every political arena to capture how they shape interactions between actors. Every chapter of this book documented how actors, at selected levels of governance, participate in and negotiate the new farmland investment game. As this book demonstrates, global investment dynamics are interwoven with other international and national economic development initiatives – socio-economic development strategies, land formalization and policies – and with numerous local political and economic dynamics, that are themselves embedded within the socio-historical trajectory of the host countries. CAS is thus a multi-level analytical tool that fosters our understanding of governance dynamics, and how they are imbricated and interdependent. CAS also helps us to understand and explain why in similar institutional environments, we may find divergent investments' outcomes or trajectories. Therefore, it is a well-adapted tool to analyse similar investment dynamics in other developing countries.

As already stated, each empirical chapter of this book focused on a specific set of actors' interactions, in a circumscribed political arena, examining in detail the co-constitutive interplay between contingencies, structure and actors' agency that has shaped them. Each chapter is thus independent, resulting from my use of a magnifying glass to explain why and how actors interact the way they do in specific situations at determined levels of governance. Yet, although analytically useful, the separation between these levels of governance, and hence these empirical chapters, is somewhat artificial. In real life, all those actors' interactions are synergetic, dynamic, adaptive, co-constitutive, reactive to each other, always changing in time and space. Therefore, all these interactions, between and within each level, are interdependent.

Chapter 2 introduced the issue of land grabbing by situating it on the international scene. It also proposed a reflection on the structuring effect of international mainstream narratives. It argued that they have a lasting shaping impact on how we think development, investment, and agriculture. Leaving them unquestioned put us at risk of not being able to think outside the box and conceive alternative visions of what socio-economic and agricultural development could be in developing countries. For instance, is the agricultural productivist model best suited to reform SSA agricultural sector with the environmental challenges of the twenty-first century? This chapter also cautions against the unforeseen impacts of international agendas that provide rationale and legitimacy to various contentious political actions at the national level regarding land policies, formalization and investment. Indeed, Chapters 4 to 7 all illustrated to some extent how actors subvert, modify, instrumentalize such narratives for other purposes. Lastly, Chapter 2 also calls for the need of politicizing the 'investors' as a group of actors to capture their motivations to invest and better understand the local impacts of their investment.

Chapter 4 analysed land policies and related politics at the national level. It highlighted that actors' interactions in relation to new farmland investments participate to the process of state formation. It is through them that state officials at central and local levels reinforce their authority towards local communities and investors, thereby (re)producing relations of domination and political subjects. Chapters 5 and 6 both adopted a local perspective to capture the impacts associated with new farmland investments in district political arenas. More specifically, Chapter 6 highlighted the importance of not overstating the authority of the central state, rather insisting on the key role played by intermediaries in Rufiji district. In it, I documented how institutional change had direct consequences on the way local bureaucrats and a local state agency conduct their activities. This interplay between structure and actors' agency transforms interactions between actors, thereby also shaping the resulting local outcomes. It is a dynamic and interactive process. Each level of governance has its own set of interactions that develop through time, with this perpetual interplay between new contingencies, structure and actors' actions. Chapter 6 sought to capture how a specific investment has restructured the local political agrarian economy in Missenyi district. I argued that Kagera Sugar safeguards its operational profitability through its participation and the reproduction of clientelistic relations of power. Its arrival led to the emergence of many new local patrons who used their position to benefit and foster their own material interests at villagers' expense. Lastly, Chapter 7 used a micro perspective, examining the political dynamics associated with investors-related land conflicts in a village in Missenyi district. I compared and explained why the leaders' reactions to these conflicts vary, highlighting that the same local context may produce different CASs.

There are many lessons learned from this analysis that can help us to better study and understand the local impacts associated with the arrival of new farmland investors in developing countries. First, the farmland investment game is lucrative and consequently, highly political. Political collusion in land acquisitions and land matters is common in Tanzania. Unsurprisingly, the general trend is that most of the benefits associated with new farmland investments, the commodification of land and the increase of capital flows are captured by government officials and political elites. Farmland investments are also directly associated with politicized processes of land formalization and land commodification. All chapters document to some extent how authority over land (or infrastructural relations of power) is key to negotiate inclusion within those new land investment dynamics (and associated clientelistic relations of power). Despite the incorporation of international narratives on investment, agricultural and socio-economic development, and land formalization to protect the poor's land rights into Tanzanian land policies and discourses, development objectives are consistently not achieved in Tanzania. Rather, as this book shows, the implementation process of such policies is often subverted by various government officials and elites who use them to strengthen their authority over land, dispossess villagers and position themselves with investors.

Second, at least in the Tanzanian case, clientelistic relations of power are pervasive and determinant of interactions between actors, and of the observed outcomes associated with the studied investment projects. As demonstrated in Chapter 4, Magufuli and his government's actions must be understood against constraining effects of political factionalism, and of the clientelistic nature of the prevailing Tanzanian political settlement. Political power in Tanzania is also much about controlling clientelistic networks. Similarly, in Chapter 5, I discussed how local state officials and intermediaries sought to strengthen their position of authority to capture some of the benefits associated with the arrival of new investors in the district. They navigate the structure and subvert central institutions to foster their material interests. Interestingly, the importance of material interests and of establishing clientelistic interactions with new investors to establish their political authority remain unquestioned. It means that at the local level too, clientelistic relations of power are heavily constraining: not only do they shape actors' interactions and practices, but they are also constitutive of the normative structure that partly shapes their interpretation of the social world. Chapter 6 also illustrated this point by highlighting that clientelistic relations of power had a very pervasive local effect, restructuring the whole local agrarian political economy. As I have argued, clientelistic relations are further crucial for investors because they can become a matter of survival: the cooptation of local elites and officials was decisive for Kagera Sugar to maintain its operational profitability. Chapter 7 argued that clientelistic relations may also have an impact on identity-building. In the first conflict, local leaders were angry of being dispossessed, and denounced collusion dynamics between Narco-associated investors and district officials. Yet, when the opportunity came along, they grasped it. To partake the clientelistic game at play, local leaders discriminated against and excluded a sub-set of villagers, the migrants.

Third, not all actors are equal in their capacity to grasp investment-induced opportunities to renegotiate the structural constraints they endure. As already mentioned, actors' capacity to negotiate these structural components depends on how much power they already hold within a given institutional setting. Although theoretically everyone has this capacity to negotiate, pre-existing structural inequalities affect actors' power within a given CAS. Indeed, my empirical findings revealed that actors who hold more power, such as government officials, local and national political elites, and investors had the greatest capacity to renegotiate the social structure to foster their political and material interests. For instance, in Chapters 5 and 6, I showed that new farmland investments created opportunities, mostly grasped by state officials at both the central and local governance levels to produce their political authority. Their institutional position favoured them to access/create new accumulation opportunities associated with the commodification of land and new capital flows. In addition, as Chapter 4 demonstrated, actors who hold a great amount of political power, such as the President, have a greater flexibility not only in navigating institutional constraints, but also in innovating institutionally. Power holding is also contingent as Chapter 7 demonstrates: even village leaders, when the opportunity arises, may use their authority at the expense of others. Lastly, this book also shows that specific local actors – and not necessarily the most powerful – such as district officials win almost every time, at least more than all the others. Although their place in the institutional architecture is decisive, their capacity and ability to exert their agency is crucial: these district officials may have known better than others how to play their cards in this new Tanzanian farmland investment game. Other actors, namely local communities and more specifically women, youths and migrants, also have some bargaining powers. They might have a poor hand, but they are learning to play their cards right. Yet their odds of losing are greater because they always start playing the game with much less cards than their adversaries.

Fourth, the nature of interactions between levels of governance, collaborative or competitive, is key in determining the local outcomes associated with new investments. As explained in Chapter 5, the fact that local officials acted as state brokers negatively impacted the relationship investors developed with local communities. Bypassing local communities may be consequential: it may impede the capacity of the investor to start production. However, competitive interactions between actors at the central and local governance levels may open possibilities for local communities to protect and safeguard their land rights as I have also demonstrated in this chapter. But then, this outcome is contingent on the nature of actors' interactions at the micro-level. It is possible only if local leaders favour transparent governance procedures, and are accountable to villagers. In Missenyi district, the absence of intermediaries, a protected domestic market, and the collaborative interactions between the investor and central government officials have allowed Kagera Sugar to use existing and create new clientelistic relations to protect its profitability. It led to mixed local outcomes. The absence of intermediaries tended to influence positively the relationship this investor developed with local communities which is mostly collaborative. In return for contributing to local development projects, infrastructural development and providing employment, the company needs villages' collaboration for its new land acquisitions, and their economic participation as contractual and occasional labour. Yet clientelistic relations and the cooptation process of local elites also had negative impacts on local communities. They led to the emergence of many new local patrons who fostered their own material interests at their expense. Therefore, transformations in the agrarian political economy induced by Kagera Sugar triggered local political schemes that led to land conflicts, land dispossession and social marginalization within local communities.

Fifth, investments' impacts are locally differentiated and tend to reinforce pre-existing exclusion dynamics. Capturing and differentiating the local impacts of investment within a given community and even within a given familial unit requires empirical inquiry. We should be cautious with aggregated numbers and how we interpret them. For instance, an increase on household revenues does not mean that every household member benefits. Again, it depends on the dynamics pertaining to every household. Many women I have interviewed in Kagera region have found their situation worsening with the arrival of Kagera Sugar: now, they are cultivating the familial plot alone and taking care of the family's expenses without benefiting from their husband's new revenue. In fact, as I have tried to do in Chapter 6, to capture the extent of the local impacts in each setting, we need to broaden our field of inquiry to capture not only the direct but also the indirect effects of those investments. However, this is not an easy undertaking. For instance, there is still much to investigate to understand the gendered impacts of such investments, and it is an important limitation of this book which has not tackled this question directly.

Sixth, the lack of local accountability is an important problem. Regardless of villagers' consent, in Tanzania, village land is increasingly leased to new investors. Yet, in my opinion, villagers are the first instance to whom those investors should be accountable because they are in the best position to monitor them. They should have the power to either take back their land or lease it to another investor if investors do not fulfil their promises. Given this, the recentralization of land management that is underway in Tanzania is highly counter-productive. It increases the number of players in the game, and as we have seen, their prime motivation is not always of ensuring that villagers receive benefits from the investment. The presence of intermediaries also gives room to political manoeuvres and land transactions that lack transparency, which may protect in the end unproductive and incompetent investors at villagers' expense as this book shows. Whatever its claims, faced with this land rush, the Tanzanian state has failed to protect villagers' land rights and to ensure lasting local socio-economic development. Moreover, the Tanzanian government's more recent actions regarding land investment and land management do not indicate that a new direction is envisioned.

Seventh, unquestioning mainstream narratives on agricultural and economic development and investment have lasting and dramatic consequences for the peasantry of developing countries. Peasants have the most at stake and risk losing it all. They are stuck between a rock and a hard place, in-between global development orientations and the political economy prevailing in their country. Their land is being targeted by many powerful actors who dismissed them as significant actors and portray the way they use their land and natural resources as unsustainable and unproductive. If poverty reduction and socio-economic development are really the priorities in SSA, seriously questioning those assumptions and acknowledging their effects at the local level is crucial. These global narratives are shaping investment and development projects in a way that risks hurting more than helping those who should benefit from them. Until then, it should not be a surprise that peasants remain suspicious and keep resisting these grand development agendas. As Vercillo and Hird-Younger (2019, p. 764) put it: '[…] [peasants] make rational choices based on experiences of historical antecedence, including decades of failed development projects, elite corruption and mismanagement, degrading ecologies and donor hegemony'.

As a final concluding remark, I want to mention that I have used socio-economic and political analytical lenses to examine how the arrival of new investors impacted local dynamics. Although relevant, this focus led me to overlook other key dimensions such as environment or health issues associated with new farmland investment projects in developing countries. These dimensions are also eminently political. New domination mechanisms related to health issues and environmental changes might generate new mobilizations of those who are excluded-weakened-marginalized, or new incentives for actors to transform the prevailing social structure to foster their interests. Kagera Sugar is a case in point. I disregarded many consequences associated with the arrival of the company. For instance, although the company provides water for free, water is often contaminated with chemical products and fertilizers that are used to treat sugarcane. There is to my knowledge no study of how it impacts the health of local communities drinking it, or the quality and nutritional value of the staple crops they are growing. In addition, even if the company has built roads that facilitated transportation and fostered socio-economic development, most of these new roads are not made of concrete.

They are highly compact sand roads. Concretely, when trucks carrying sugarcane are circulating, considerable amount of dust is raised from the ground, polluting, and deteriorating the air local communities are breathing. Moreover, even if the introduction of sugarcane production had positive impacts in fostering and developing the local economy of Missenyi district, this local focus on sugarcane affected the food security of those communities. In case of important drought – as it was the case in the Fall 2016/Winter 2017 when there was no rainy season – there was a shortage of food in the whole district. The situation was judged critical enough for district officials to pass a special law forbidding people from selling food outside the district as a desperate measure to contain the situation. Sugarcane is not a staple food. I could not help but think at that moment that if the company had grown maize instead, and used its irrigation capacity to this end, starvation would have been avoided. Thus, future research should consider environmental and health impacts of such farmland projects, including a critical analysis of the choice of commercial crops that are favoured. Collaborative and interdisciplinary research that would integrate these aspects alongside a socio-economic and political analysis such as the one I have done in this research project would nuance and further expand our understanding of the transformation on local dynamics induced by these new investment dynamics.

Notes

Chapter 1

1   The national level refers to national policies that affect the whole country. The local level refers to the district as an administrative division in Tanzania, which usually comprises between fifty and seventy villages. The micro-level refers to the administrative unit of a village.

2   In addition to participant and nonparticipant observation, I conducted over 250 semi-structured and open interviews with various stakeholders, i.e. government officials, local leaders, farmers, villagers, civil society organizations and local and international investors. I conducted the interviews with government officials and investors alone, but I hired a Tanzanian research assistant to work with me while conducting interviews with local communities. In order to protect confidentiality, and ensure my informants' safety, the investors, villages and sub-villages names have been anonymized.

3   Although this contention on relations of power may appear deterministic, it is worth noting that my claim is not that they are exotic or permanent features of the Tanzanian political configuration. Rather, my contention is that they might be, during a given period, consistent, transversal, preeminent and significantly shaping actors' interactions.

4   The CCM has been the Party in power in Tanzania since Independence.

Chapter 2

1   Several scholars have criticized and nuanced this dominant narrative. For instance, it is true that those global crises played a role in this global trend towards the financialization of the agricultural sector. However, and importantly, land grabs are not a new phenomenon in many countries, and land issues are embedded within national institutional and historical legacies. In addition, we do know now that investors are coming from everywhere and for various reasons. Furthermore, many recent publications have stressed the importance of domestic

investors (Jayne et al., 2016, 2019; Lusasi, Pedersen and Friis-Hansen, 2019; Cochrane and Andrews, 2021).

2   Simply defined, a cash trap refers to the gap in time between paying suppliers and receiving payments from sales, which impacts available cash flows.

3   The investment climate is difficult for reasons that include long and overlapping bureaucratic procedures, corruption issues, risky political context, unsecure land rights, lack of infrastructural development and limited national markets. Often, land is acquired in remote and underdeveloped areas that have no electricity and water, and only poorly developed roads that do not allow regular commercial transportation.

4   Those tacit political agreements refer to deals that investors have secretly concluded with the Russian government: 'with the Kremlin, which seems to have promised not to investigate the dubious practices of the oligarchs in return for their investment in the countryside' (Boldyrev, 2001, p. 21 in Visser, Mamonova and Spoor, 2012, p. 912).

5   The Tanzanian Investment Centre (TIC) was created in 1997 by the Tanzania Investment Act. TIC is mostly an investment facilitator, and it aims to encourage investments in the country by attracting foreign investors and promoting Tanzania as a business-friendly country. In addition to offering fiscal advantages to investors, TIC supports and facilitates obtainment of all necessary licenses and permits. Also, TIC has created a land bank which in theory allows the agency to match available land to investor's needs. The parcels of land included in this land bank are generally claimed free from local conflicts because the land has already been transferred from village land to general land.

6   This investment is also discussed in Chapter 5.

Chapter 3

1   For example, fertilizer subsidies were completely abolished in 1994–5.

Chapter 4

1   There were two Mkukuta. Mkukuta I covers the period 2005–10, and Mkukuta II covers 2010–15.

2 It is important to note that I do not imply here that villagers are passive victims of higher authorities. My findings show that despite their limited powers, they also resist and subvert official policies. However, I do not discuss this aspect in this chapter because my focus is on state officials' practices.

Chapter 5

1 My analysis identifies two distinct groups of local bureaucrats in Rufiji district: district officials and Rubada officials. These local bureaucrats are appointed, paid and accountable to the central state. This contrasts with village leaders in Tanzania, who are elected by villagers and are unpaid.

2 Numerous compensation issues are worth mentioning. First, The compensation process started only in 2013, so about nine years after the eviction of farmers. Second, only people living near the main road were offered compensation, the others were simply ignored. Third, the amount offered by the company to farmers was ridiculously low, and the loss of land itself was not compensated (fieldnotes and interviews villagers Rufiji district, 2016).

3 Investor is the same as Investor Z discussed in Chapter 2.

4 My research assistant conducted a follow-up visit to the farm in January 2020. Although the road and infrastructure such as bridges have not been improved, he witnessed some development on the farmland itself. For instance, the investor has purchased two recent commercial tractors, four boats (for transportation during the flooding period) and has built a garage, two new houses and a small recreation centre. Solar energy installations now provide electricity. In addition, since 2019, rice growing has started on a small portion of the land, but the harvest was lost because of inadequate rainfall during seeding. It is difficult to interpret the motivations behind these developments (see discussion on Investor Z in Chapter 2).

5 The most important of those projects were: The Rufiji mechanized cultivation scheme (British colonial period 1948–56); the Rufiji Basin Survey (FAO – 1953); the Stiegler Gorge project (Tanzanian government and the Norwegian Agency for Development Cooperation (NORAD) 1971–84) (see Hoag, 2003).

6 It should be noted here that the Rufiji hydropower project has been revived under Magufuli's presidency to increase the electricity supply countrywide. The Tanzania Electric Supply Company (TANESCO) is undertaking the ambitious

project of an estimated cost of about US$ 4 billion. Construction officially started in June 2019 (expected completion date in 2022). TANESCO has contracted Eslwedy Technology and Arab contractors, two Egyptian companies, to build the mega-infrastructure. The project is controversial because the involved costs are likely to be underestimated and for its potential destructive effect of the Selous Game Reserve, one of the Africa's largest protected natural reserves. Whether this project will be successful or not remains to be seen.

Chapter 6

1   The lack of transparency surrounding Kagera Sugar's land acquisitions makes it difficult to assess the exact number of hectares owned by the company.
2   Other scholars have observed similar processes of social differentiation leading to the emergence of a new middle class in other regions of Tanzania (Cooksey, 2012; Sulle, 2017; Bluwstein et al., 2018; Jayne et al., 2019).
3   The relationship between new farmland investments and land dispossession has been well documented in the Tanzanian context (Abdallah et al., 2014; Bergius, Benjaminsen and Widgren, 2017; Chung, 2017; Engström, Bélair and Blache, 2018).
4   See The Local Government (Urban Authorities) Act 1982 and the Local Government Laws (Miscellaneous Amendments) Act 1999.

Chapter 7

1   Other scholars have observed and documented instances in which ethnic identity becomes politically salient in Tanzania (Kelsall 2000; Gibbon 2001; Must 2018; Becker 2020).
2   In addition, the *mukama* (the King) had exclusive prerogatives regarding land, which were instated through what was known as the *nyarubanja* system. *Nyarubanja* is the category of land that was under the King's control. Because he became the owner of land without heirs, and could transfer individual/ clan land to *nyarubanja*, the king used land allocation to enforce client–patron relationships and ensure political stability. As Reining (1962, p. 66) explains: '[The king could single] out a block of *bibanja* and their occupants [...] designating them tenants of his appointee'. In this way, Haya landowners became

tenants of the King's political appointee, and political appointees, clients of the King. Land attribution through this *nyarubanja* system was significant: estimates are that about 20 per cent of Haya land was allocated in form of royal gifts. The remaining land (about 10 per cent) was subject to the market system, sold and bought by interested buyers and sellers (Reining, 1962).

3   The proliferation of investors is not the only factor having contributed to this pressure to formalize and title land. Land formalization programmes are also resulting from collaborative international and national development projects (see discussion in Chapter 2).

4   As noted by Kelsall (2000), the phenomenon of districtization in Tanzania is associated with competitive politics that have created incentives for local politicians to secure strong local support. Indeed, under Tanzania's multi-party constitution, to sit in the cabinet, an MP must secure election in a constituency. Thus, 'the tendency is for a closer linking of the national and local levels, and the increasing relevance of local concerns to national policy' (Kelsall, 2000, p. 552).

5   Politically, Tanzania is divided into constituencies. During national elections, each constituency elects an MP.

6   As showed in Chapter 3, struggles between political factions within the ruling elite are an important feature of Tanzanian politics (Cooksey and Kelsall, 2011; Gray, 2015; Eriksen, 2018; Tsubura, 2018).

7   The conflict had not been resolved as of 2017, and the land transfer was still in the administrative process.

References

Abate, A. G. (2020) "The effects of land grabs on peasant households: The case of the floriculture sector in Oromia, Ethiopia", *African Affairs*, 119(1), pp. 90–114. doi: 10.1093/afraf/adz008.

Abdallah, J. et al. (2014) "Large-scale land acquisitions in Tanzania: A critical analysis of practices and dynamics", in Kaag, M. and Zoomers, A. (eds) *The global land grab: Beyond the hype*. Chicago: Zed Books, pp. 36–53.

Agribusiness country diagnostic Tanzania (2016). Global agriculture and food security program (GAFSP). London, England: Cambridge Economic Policy Associates Ltd.

Aha, B. and Ayitey, J. Z. (2017) "Biofuels and the hazards of land grabbing: Tenure (in)security and indigenous farmers' investment decisions in Ghana", *Land Use Policy; Kidlington*, 60, pp. 48–59.

Ahmed, A., Campion, B. B. and Gasparatos, A. (2017) "Biofuel development in Ghana: Policies of expansion and drivers of failure in the jatropha sector", *Renewable and Sustainable Energy Reviews*, 70, pp. 133–149. doi: 10.1016/j. rser.2016.11.216.

Ahmed, A., Campion, B. B. and Gasparatos, A. (2019) "Towards a classification of the drivers of jatropha collapse in Ghana elicited from the perceptions of multiple stakeholders", *Sustainability Science*, 14, pp. 315–339.

Akram-Lodhi, A. H. (2007) "Land, markets and neoliberal enclosure: An agrarian political economy perspective", *Third World Quarterly*, 28(8), pp. 1437–1456.

Akram-Lodhi, A. H. and Kay, C. (2010) "Surveying the agrarian question (part 2): Current debates and beyond", *The Journal of Peasant Studies*, 37(2), pp. 255–284. doi: 10.1080/03066151003594906.

Al Jazeera (2020) "Tanzania opposition loses key seats in vote marred by fraud claim", 29 October. Available at: https://www.aljazeera.com/news/2020/10/29/tanzania-opposition-loses-key-seats-in-vote-marred-by-fraud-claim (Accessed: 17 June 2021).

Alhassan, S. I., Shaibu, M. T. and Kuwornu, J. K. M. (2018) "Is land grabbing an opportunity or a menace to development in developing countries? Evidence from Ghana", *Local Environment*, 23(12), pp. 1121–1140. doi: 10.1080/13549839.2018.1531839.

Anaafo, D. and Guba, B. (2017) "Do land reforms have adverse impacts on the livelihoods of poor land users? Evidence from the Nkoranza South Municipality, Ghana", *Canadian Journal of African* Studies, 51(2), pp. 293–318. doi: 10.1080/00083968.2017.1303390.

Andreoni, A. (2017) "Anti-corruption in Tanzania: A political settlements analysis". ACE, Anti-corruption evidence working paper 1.

Anseeuw, W. and Boche, M. (2015) "South Africa in African agriculture: Investment models and their dynamics towards a structured conquest", *Autrepart*, 76(4), pp. 49–66.

Anseeuw, W., Boche, M., Breu, T., Giger, M., Lay, J., Messerli, P. and Nolte, K. (2012) "Transnational land deals for agriculture in the global south. Analytical report based on the land matrix database". CDE/CIRAD/GIGA, Bern/Montpellier/Hamburg.

Antonelli, M. et al. (2015) "Global investments in agricultural land and the role of the EU: Drivers, scope and potential impacts", *Land Use Policy*, 47, pp. 98–111. doi: 10.1016/j.landusepol.2015.04.007.

Antwi-Bediako, R. et al. (2019) "Global investment failures and transformations: A review of hyped jatropha spaces", *Sustainability*, 11(3371), pp. 1–23.

Arnall, A. (2019) "'Employment until the end of the world': Exploring the role of manipulation in a Mozambican land deal", *Land Use Policy*, 81, pp. 862–870.

Attah, N. E. (2021) "Behind accumulation and dispossession: State and large-scale agricultural land investments in Nigeria", in Cochrane, L. and Andrews, N. (eds) *The transnational land rush in Africa, A decade after the spike*. Cham, Switzerland: Palgrave MacMillan (International political economy series), pp. 113–138.

Ayelazuno, J. A. (2019) "Land governance for extractivism and capitalist farming in Africa: An overview", *Land Use Policy*, 81, pp. 843–851. doi: 10.1016/j.landusepol.2018.06.037.

Ayoade, J. A. A. (1988) "States without citizens", in Rotchild, D. and Chazan, N. (eds) *The precarious balance*. United States: Westview Press Inc., pp. 100–118.

Badiey, N. (2013) "The strategic instrumentalization of land tenure in 'state-building': The case of Juba, South Sudan", *Africa: The Journal of the International African Institute*, 83(1), pp. 57–77.

Baumgartner, P. et al. (2015) "Impacts of large-scale land investments on income, prices, and employment: Empirical analyses in Ethiopia", *World Development*, 72, pp. 175–190.

Bayart, J.-F. (1989) *L'Etat en Afrique: La politique du ventre*. Paris: Fayard.

Bayart, J.-F., Geschiere, P. and Nyamnjoh, F. (2001) "Autochtonie, démocratie et citoyenneté en Afrique", *Critique internationale*, 10, pp. 177–194.

BBC News (2020a) "Coronavirus: John Magufuli declares Tanzania free of Covid-19", 8 June. Available at: https://www.bbc.com/news/world-africa-52966016 (Accessed: 17 June 2021).

BBC News (2020b) "Coronavirus: Tanzania hospitals overwhelmed", 12 May. Available at: https://www.bbc.com/news/world-africa-52646640 (Accessed: 17 June 2021).

Becker, F. (2020) "Locating the 'Customary' in post-colonial Tanzania's politics: The shifting modus operandi of the rural state", *Journal of Eastern African Studies*, 14(1), p. 145163. https://doi.org/10.1080/17531055.2019.1711311.

Behuria, P., Buur, L. and Gray, H. (2017) "Studying political settlements in Africa", *African Affairs*, 116(464), pp. 508–525. doi: 10.1093/afraf/adx019.

Bélair, J. (2019) *Farmland investments in Tanzania: A local perspective on the political economy of agri-food projects*. Ottawa, Canada: University of Ottawa.

Bennett, J. (2005) "The agency of assemblages and the North American blackout", *Public Culture*, 17(3), pp. 445–466. doi: 10.1215/08992363-17-3-445.

Berger, P. L. and Luckmann, T. (1968) *The social construction of reality*. London, England: Penguin Books.

Berger, R. (2015) "Now I see it, now I don't: Researcher's position and reflexivity in qualitative research", *Qualitative Research*, 15(2), pp. 219–234.

Bergius, M., Benjaminsen, T. A. and Widgren, M. (2017) "Green economy, Scandinavian investments and agricultural modernization in Tanzania", *Journal of Peasant Studies*, 45, pp. 825–852.

Bernstein, H. (2010). *Class dynamics of agrarian change*. Halifax: Fernwood Publishing; Sterling, Virginia: Kumarian Press.

Berry, S. (1993) *No condition is Permanent: The social dynamics of agrarian change in Sub-Saharan Africa*. Madison, Wisconsin, United States: University of Wisconsin Press (ACLS Humanities E-Book).

Bluwstein, J. et al. (2018) "Between dependence and deprivation: The interlocking nature of land alienation in Tanzania", *Journal of Agrarian Change*, 18(4), pp. 806–830.

Boamah, F. (2014) "How and why chiefs formalise land use in recent times: The politics of land dispossession through biofuels investments in Ghana", *Review of African Political Economy; London*, 41(141), p. 406.

Boamah, F. and Overå, R. (2016) "Rethinking livelihood impacts of biofuel land deals in Ghana", *Development & Change*, 47(1), pp. 98–129. doi: 10.1111/dech.12213.

Boche, M. and Anseeuw, W. (2017) "Accès au foncier et relations de pouvoir: l'enchâssement des acquisitions foncières à grande échelle au Mozambique", *Géographie, Economie, Société*, 19(3), pp. 377–401.

Boone, C. (2014) *Property and political order in Africa*. New York: Cambridge University Press.

Boone, C. and Nyeme, L. (2015) "Land institutions and political ethnicity in Africa: Evidence from Tanzania", *Comparative Politics*, 48(1), pp. 67–86.

Borras, S. (2011) "Global land grabbing and trajectories of agrarian change: A preliminary analysis", *Journal of Agrarian Change*, 12(1), pp. 34–59.

Borras, S. M. B. and Franco, J. C. (2013) "Global land grabbing and political reactions 'From below'", *Third World Quarterly*, 34(9), pp. 1723–1747. doi: 10.1080/01436597.2013.843845.

Bräutigam, D. and Zhang, H. (2013) "Green dreams: Myth and reality in China's agricultural investment in Africa", *Third World Quarterly*, 34(9), pp. 1676–1696. doi: 10.1080/01436597.2013.843846.

Brent, Z. W. (2015) "Territorial restructuring and resistance in Argentina", *The Journal of Peasant Studies*, 42(3–4), pp. 671–694. doi: 10.1080/03066150.2015.1013100.

Brewin, D. (2016) "2015 elections & results", *Tanzanian Affairs*. Issue 113, Politics, 1 January. Available at: www.tzaffairs.org/2016/01/2015-elections-results (Accessed: 10 March 2019).

Bromwich, B. (2017) "Power, contested institutions and land: Repoliticising analysis of natural resources and conflict in Darfur", *Journal of Eastern African Studies*, 12(1), pp. 1–21. doi: 10.1080/17531055.2017.1403782.

Brüntrup, M. et al. (2016) "Large-scale agricultural investments and rural development in Tanzania: Lessons learned, steering requirements and policy responses". 2016 World Bank Conference on Land and Poverty. Available at: https://www.die-gdi.de/uploads/media/Bruentrup-230-230_paper.pdf.

Brüntrup, M. et al. (2018) "Nucleus-outgrower schemes as an alternative to traditional smallholder agriculture in Tanzania – strengths, weaknesses and policy requirements", *Food Security*, 10(4), pp. 807–826. doi: 10.1007/s12571-018-0797-0.

"The bulldozer's light tread" (2016) *Africa Confidential*, 57(23). https://www.africa-confidential.com/article-preview/id/11831/The_bulldozer%27s_light_tread.

Burnod, P., Gingembre, M. and Ratsialonana, R. (2013) "Competition over authority and access: International land deals in Madagascar", *Development & Change*, 44(2), pp. 357–379.

Buur, L., Nystrand, M. J. and Pedersen, R. H. (2017) "The political economy of land and natural resource investments in Africa: An analytical framework", *DIIS. Danish Institute for International Studies*, DISS Working Paper 2017, 2, pp. 1–48.

Carlson, R. G. (1993) "Symbolic mediation and commoditization: A critical examination of alcohol use among the Haya of Bukoba, Tanzania", *Medical Anthropology*, 15(1), pp. 41–62. doi: 10.1080/01459740.1992.9966081.

Castellanos-Navarrete, A. and Jansen, K. (2015) "Oil palm expansion without enclosure: Smallholders and environmental narratives", *The Journal of Peasant Studies*, 42(3–4), pp. 791–816. doi: 10.1080/03066150.2015.1016920.

"CCM springs surprise" (2015) *Africa Confidential*, 56(15). https://www.africa-confidential.com/article-preview/id/11164/CCM_springs_surprise

Christiaensen, L. (2017) "Agriculture in Africa – Telling myths from facts: A synthesis", *Food Policy*, 67, pp. 1–11. doi: 10.1016/j.foodpol.2017.02.002.

Chung, Y. B. (2017) "Engendering the new enclosures: Development, involuntary resettlement and the struggles for social reproduction in Coastal Tanzania", *Development and Change*, 48(1), pp. 98–120. doi: 10.1111/dech.12288.

The Citizen (2021) "President Samia outlines stimulus plan", 23 April. Available at: https://www.thecitizen.co.tz/tanzania/news/-president-samia-outlines-stimulus-plan-3373802 (Accessed: 17 June 2021).

Clapp, J. (2014) "Financialization, distance and global food politics", *The Journal of Peasant Studies*, 41(5), pp. 798–814.

Cliffe, L. (1975) *Rural cooperation in Tanzania*. Dar es Salaam, Tanzania: Tanzania Pub.House.

Cochrane, L. and Andrews, N. (eds) (2021) *The transnational land rush in Africa, A decade after the spike*. Cham, Switzerland: Palgrave MacMillan (International political economy series).

Collier, P. and Venables, A. J. (2012) "Land deals in Africa: Pioneers and speculators", *Journal of Globalization and Development*, 3(1), pp. 1–20. doi: 10.1515/1948-1837.1228.

Constant Martin, D. (1988) *Tanzania, l'invention d'une culture politique*. Paris: Presses de la Fondation nationale des sciences politiques: Karthala.

Cooksey, B. (2012) "Politics, patronage and projects: The political economy of agricultural policy in Tanzania". *Future Agricultures*, Working Paper 040.

Cooksey, B. (2017) "IPTL, Richmond and 'Escrow': The price of private power procurement in Tanzania". Africa Research Institute. Available at: https://www.africaresearchinstitute.org/newsite/publications/iptl-richmond-escrow-price-private-power-procurement-tanzania/#three (Accessed: 11 March 2019).

Cooksey, B. and Kelsall, T. (2011) *The political economy of the investment climate in Tanzania*. Research Report 01, Africa Power and Politics Programme (APPP). Overseas Development Institute.

Côté, I. and Mitchell, M. I. (2017) "Deciphering 'sons of the soil' conflicts: A critical survey of the literature", *Ethnopolitics*, 16(4), pp. 333–351. doi: 10.1080/17449057.2015.1089050.

Cramer, C. et al. (2016) "Mistakes, crises, and research independence: The perils of fieldwork as a form of evidence", *African Affairs*, 115(458), pp. 145–160. doi: 10.1093/afraf/adv067.

Davis, B., Di Giuseppe, S. and Zezza, A. (2017) "Are African households (not) leaving agriculture? Patterns of households' income sources in rural Sub-Saharan Africa", *Food Policy*, 67, pp. 153–174.

De Schutter, O. (2011) "How not to think of land-grabbing: Three critiques of large-scale investments in farmland", *The Journal of Peasant Studies*, 38(2), pp. 249–279.

Deane, K. and Stevano, S. (2016) "Towards a political economy of the use of research assistants: Reflections from fieldwork in Tanzania and Mozambique", *Qualitative Research*, 16(2), pp. 213–228. doi: 10.1177/1468794115578776.

Deininger, K. and Byerlee, D. (2011) "Rising global interest in farmland: Can it yield sustainable and equitable benefits?" Washington, DC: World Bank Publications.

Deininger, K. and Xia, F. (2018) "Assessing the long-term performance of large-scale land transfers: Challenges and opportunities in Malawi's estate sector", *World Development*, 104, pp. 281–296. doi: 10.1016/j.worlddev.2017.11.025.

Dell'Angelo, J. et al. (2017) "The tragedy of the grabbed commons: Coercion and dispossession in the global land rush", *World Development*, 92, pp. 1–12. doi: 10.1016/j.worlddev.2016.11.005.

Di Matteo, F. and Schoneveld, G. C. (2016) "Working Paper 201. Agricultural investments in Mozambique: An analysis of investment trends, business models and social and environmental conduct". Center for International Forestry Research (CIFOR). doi: 10.17528/cifor/005958.

Dunn, K. C. (2009) "'Sons of the soil' and contemporary state making: Autochthony, uncertainty and political violence in Africa", *Third World Quarterly*, 30(1), pp. 113–127. doi: 10.1080/01436590802622417.

The Economist Intelligence Unit (2010) "The political scene: Change is taking place within the CCM", 7 October. Available at: http://country.eiu.com/article.aspx?artic leid=1397519124&Country=Tanzania (Accessed: 18 March 2019).

Edelman, M. (2013) "Messy hectares: Questions about the epistemology of land grabbing data", *The Journal of Peasant Studies*, 40(3), pp. 485–501. doi: 10.1080/03066150.2013.801340.

Ekeh, P. P. (1975) "Colonialism and the two publics in Africa: A theoretical statement", *Comparative Studies in Society and History*, 17(1), pp. 91–112.

Elias, P. (2015) "Kampeni: Magufuli apiga 'push-up' nne", *Mwananchi*, 23 September. Available at: http://www.mwananchi.co.tz/habari/KAMPENI--Magufuli-apiga--push-up--nne/-/1597578/2881988/-/format/xhtml/-/ohy0w7/-/index.html (Accessed: 18 July 2017).

Engström, L. (2018) *Development delayed. Exploring the failure of a large-scale agricultural investment in Tanzania to deliver promised outcomes.* Ph.D. Acta Universitatis Agriculturae Sueciae.

Engström, L., Bélair, J. and Blache, A. (2018) "Conceptualizing dispossession in the global land rush: An aggregated analysis of four regions of Tanzania", in *African Studies Association UK (ASAUK)*, Birmingham, England.

Engström, L. and Hajdu, F. (2018) "Conjuring 'Win-world' – resilient development narratives in a large-scale agro-investment in Tanzania", *The Journal of Development Studies*, 55(6), pp. 1201–1220. doi: 10.1080/00220388.2018.1438599.

Eriksen, S. S. (2018) *Tanzania: A political economy analysis*. Oslo, Norway: Norwegian Institute of International Affairs.

Ermakoff, I. (2015) "The structure of contingency", *American Journal of Sociology*, 121(1), pp. 64–125.

Exner, A. et al. (2015) "Constructing landscapes of value: Capitalist investment for the acquisition of marginal or unused land – The case of Tanzania", *Land Use Policy*, 42, pp. 652–663. doi: 10.1016/j.landusepol.2014.10.002.

Fairbairn, M. (2014) "'Like gold with yield': Evolving intersections between farmland and finance", *The Journal of Peasant Studies*, 41(5), pp. 1–19. doi: 10.1080/03066150.2013.873977.

Feintrenie, L. (2014) "Agro-industrial plantations in Central Africa, risks and opportunities", *Biodiversity and Conservation*, 23(6), pp. 1577–1589. doi: 10.1007/s10531-014-0687-5.

Ferguson, J. and Gupta, A. (2002) "Spatializing states: Toward an ethnography of neoliberal governmentality", *American Ethnologist*, 29(4), pp. 981–1002. doi: 10.1525/ae.2002.29.4.981.

Fig, D. (2011) "Agrocarburants au Mozambique: entre espoirs et déboires", *Alternatives Sud*, 18, pp. 77–90.

Fitzgerald, A. (2017) *Wearing an amulet: Land titling and tenure (in) security in Tanzania*. Maynooth, Ireland: Maynooth University.

Fogelman, C. and Bassett, T. J. (2017) "Mapping for investability: Remaking land and maps in Lesotho", *Geoforum*, 82, pp. 252–258. doi: 10.1016/j.geoforum.2016.07.008.

Fouéré, M.-A. (2011) "Tanzania: la nation à l'épreuve du postsocialisme", *Politique africaine*, 1(121), pp. 69–85.

France 24 (2021) "Tanzania's Magufuli, the 'Bulldozer' president who dismissed Covid-19", 18 March. Available at: https://www.france24.com/en/africa/20210318-tanzania-s-magufuli-the-bulldozer-president-who-dismissed-covid-19 (Accessed: 17 June 2021).

Gerlach, A.-C. and Liu, P. (2010) "Resource-seeking foreign direct investment in African agriculture". FAO Commodity and Trade Policy Research Working Paper No. 31.

Geschiere, P. and Jackson, S. (2006) "Autochthony and the crisis of citizenship: Democratization, decentralization, and the politics of belonging", *African Studies Review*, 49(2), pp. 1–7. doi: 10.1353/arw.2006.0104.

Gibbon, P. (2001) "Civil society, locality and globalization in rural Tanzania: A forty-year perspective", *Development and Change*, 32, pp. 819–844.

Giddens, A. (2004) *The constitution of society. Outline of the theory of structuration.* Cambridge: Polity Press.

Giddens, A. and Pierson, C. (1998) *Conversations with Anthony Giddens: Making sense of modernity.* Stanford, California: Stanford University Press.

Gill, B. (2016) "Can the river speak? Epistemological confrontation in the rise and fall of the land grab in Gambella, Ethiopia", *Environment and Planning A: Economy and Space*, 48(4), pp. 699–717. doi: 10.1177/0308518X15610243.

Glassman, J. (2006) "Primitive accumulation, accumulation by dispossession, accumulation by 'extra-economic' means", *Progress in Human Geography*, 30(5), pp. 608–625.

Glover, S. and Jones, S. (2019) "Can commercial farming promote rural dynamism in sub-Saharan Africa? Evidence from Mozambique", *World Development*, 114, pp. 110–121.

Goetz, A. (2015) "How different are the UK and China? Investor countries in comparative perspective", *Canadian Journal of Development Studies / Revue canadienne d'études du développement*, 36(2), pp. 179–195. doi: 10.1080/02255189.2015.1030370.

Government of Tanzania (1995) "National Land Policy 1995".

GRAIN (2016) "The global farmland grab in 2016: How big, how bad?" GRAIN. Available at: https://grain.org/article/entries/5492-the-global-farmland-grab-in-2016-how-big-how-bad (Accessed: 1 September 2021).

GRAIN (2018) "Failed farmland deals. A growing legacy of disaster and pain." GRAIN. Available at: https://mokoro.co.uk/land-rights-article/failed-farmland-deals-a-growing-legacy-of-disaster-and-pain/ (Accessed: 1 September 2021).

Gray, H. (2018-02-15). *Turbulence and order in economic development: Economic transformation in Tanzania and Vietnam.* Oxford University Press. Retrieved 12 May 2022, from https://oxford.universitypressscholarship.com/view/10.1093/oso/9780198714644.001.0001/oso-9780198714644.

Gray, H. S. (2015) "The political economy of grand corruption in Tanzania", *African Affairs*, 114(456), pp. 382–403. doi: 10.1093/afraf/adv017.

Greco, E. (2016) "Village land politics and the legacy of ujamaa", *Review of African Political Economy*, 43(sup1), pp. 22–40. doi: 10.1080/03056244.2016.1219179.

Greco, E. (2017) "Farmers or squatters? Collective land claims on Sisal Estates, Tanzania (1980s–2000s)", *Journal of Agrarian Change*, 17(1), pp. 166–187. doi: 10.1111/joac.12148.

The Guardian (2014) "Tanzania energy scandal ousts senior politicians", 24 December. Available at: https://www.theguardian.com/global-development/2014/dec/24/tanzania-energy-scandal-ousts-senior-politicians (Accessed: 10 March 2019).

Hagmann, T. and Péclard, D. (2010) "Negotiating statehood: Dynamics of power and domination in Africa", *Development and Change*, 41(4), pp. 539–562. doi: 10.1111/j.1467-7660.2010.01656.x.

Hall, D. (2013) "Primitive accumulation, accumulation by dispossession and the global land grab", *Third World Quarterly*, 34(9), pp. 1582–1604. doi: 10.1080/01436597.2013.843854.

Hall, P. A. and Taylor, R. C. R. (1996) "Political science and the three new institutionalisms", *Political Studies*, 44(5), pp. 936–957. doi: 10.1111/j.1467-9248.1996.tb00343.x.

Hall, R. et al. (2015) "Resistance, acquiescence or incorporation? An introduction to land grabbing and political reactions 'from below'", *The Journal of Peasant Studies*, 42(3–4), pp. 467–488. doi: 10.1080/03066150.2015.1036746.

Hall, R. and Kepe, T. (2017) "Elite capture and state neglect: New evidence on South Africa's land reform", *Review of African Political Economy*, 44(151), pp. 122–130. doi: 10.1080/03056244.2017.1288615.

HLPE (2011) "Land tenure and international investments in agriculture. A report by the High Level Panel of Experts on Food Security and Nutrition of the Committee on World Food Security".

Haulle, E. (2015) "Land resource in Tanzania: Whose state, whose resource?", *International Journal of Social Science Studies*, 3(6), pp. 70–78. doi: 10.11114/ijsss.v3i6.1102.

Herbst, J. I. (2000) *States and power in Africa: Comparative lessons in authority and control*. Princeton, New Jersey: Princeton University Press (Princeton studies in international history and politics).

Herrmann, R. T. (2017) "Large-scale agricultural investments and smallholder welfare: A comparison of wage labor and outgrower channels in Tanzania", *World Development*, 90, pp. 294–310. doi: http://dx.doi.org.proxy.bib.uottawa.ca/10.1016/j.worlddev.2016.10.007.

Hindeya, T. W. (2018) "An analysis of how large-scale agricultural land acquisitions in Ethiopia have been justified, implemented and opposed", *African Identities*, 16(1), pp. 18–34. doi: 10.1080/14725843.2017.1319759.

Hoag, H. J. (2003) *Designing the delta: A history of water and development in the lower Rufiji River Basin, Tanzania 1945–1985*. Boston, Massachusetts, United States: Boston University.

Hopma, J. (2015) "'Planning in the wind': The failed Jordanian agricultural investments in Sudan", *Canadian Journal of Development Studies /*

Revue canadienne d'études du développement, 36(2), pp. 196–207.
doi: 10.1080/02255189.2015.1032898.

"How real the zeal?" (2015) *Africa Confidential*, 56 (24). https://www.africa-confidential.com/article-preview/id/11365/How_real_the_zeal

Hules, M. and Singh, S. J. (2017) "India's land grab deals in Ethiopia: Food security or global politics?", *Land Use Policy*, 60, pp. 343–351.

Hyden, G. (1980) *Beyond Ujamaa in Tanzania: Underdevelopment and an uncaptured peasantry*. London: Heinemann.

Iliffe, J. (1979) *A modern history of Tanganyika*. Cambridge; New York: Cambridge University Press (African studies series, 25).

Ingle, C. R. (1970) "Compulsion and rural development in Tanzania", *Canadian Journal of African Studies / Revue Canadienne des Études Africaines*, 4(1), pp. 77–100. doi: 10.2307/483743.

Irwin, K. (2006) "Into the dark heart of ethnography: The lived ethics and inequality of intimate field relationships", *Qualitative Sociology*, 29(2), pp. 155–175. doi: 10.1007/s11133-006-9011-3.

Jacob, T. and Pedersen, R. H. (2018) "New resource nationalism? Continuity and change in Tanzania's extractive industries", *The Extractive Industries and Society*, 5(2), pp. 287–292. doi:10.1016/j.exis.2018.02.001.

Jayne, T. S. et al. (2016) *Africa's changing farmland ownership: The rise of the emergent investor farmer*. Research Paper no. 15. East Lansing, Michigan, United States: Michigan State University and IFPRI: Feed the Future Innovation Lab for Food Security Policy.

Jayne, T. S. et al. (2019) "Are medium-scale farms driving agricultural transformation in sub-Saharan Africa?", *Agricultural Economics*, 50(S1), pp. 75–95. doi: 10.1111/agec.12535.

Jean Wood, Elisabeth. (2007) "Field research during war: Ethical dilemmas", in Lauren Joseph, Matthew Mahler, and Javier Auyero (eds) *New perspectives in political ethnography*. New York: Springer, pp. 205–223.

Jimenez-Soto, E. (2021) "The political ecology of shaded coffee plantations: Conservation narratives and the everyday-lived-experience of farmworkers", *The Journal of Peasant Studies*, 48(6), pp. 1284–1303. doi:10.1080/03066150.2020.1713109.

Kaarhus, R. (2018) "Land, investments and public-private partnerships: What happened to the Beira Agricultural Growth Corridor in Mozambique?", *The Journal of Modern African Studies*, 56(1), pp. 87–112. doi: 10.1017/S0022278X17000489.

Kamndaya, S. (2016) "Magufuli's sugar headache", *The Citizen*. Available at: http://www.thecitizen.co.tz/News/1840340-3093228-lpmtehz/index.html.

Kansanga, M. M. and Luginaah, I. (2019) "Agrarian livelihoods under siege: Carbon forestry, tenure constraints and the rise of capitalist forest enclosures in Ghana", *World Development*, 113, pp. 131–142.

Karsenty, A. (2018) "Un nouveau ' Grand Jeu ' autour des terres arables du monde?", in Dhérissard, G. (ed.) *Les sols au cœur de la zone critique*. London, England: ISTE Editions, pp. 27–46.

Keene, S. et al. (2015) "A view from the top: Examining elites in large-scale land deals", *Canadian Journal of Development Studies / Revue canadienne d'études du développement*, 36(2), pp. 131–146. doi: 10.1080/02255189.2015.1044503.

Kelsall, T. (2000) "Governance, local politics and districtization in Tanzania: The 1998 arumeru tax revolt", *African Affairs*, 99(397), pp. 533–551.

Kelsall, T. (2018) "Thinking and working with political settlements. The case of Tanzania". ODI (Overseas Development Institute), Working paper 541.

Kish, Z. and Fairbairn, M. (2018) "Investing for profit, investing for impact: Moral performances in agricultural investment projects", *Environment and Planning A*, 50(3), pp. 569–588.

Knuth, S. E. (2015) "Global finance and the land grab: Mapping twenty-first century strategies", *Canadian Journal of Development Studies / Revue canadienne d'études du développement*, 36(2), pp. 163–178. doi: 10.1080/02255189.2015.1046373.

Kuns, B. and Visser, O. (2016) "Towards an agroholding typology: Differentiating large farm companies in Russia and Ukraine", in *90th Annual Conference of the Agricultural Economics Society*, University of Warwick, England.

Land Rights research and Resources institute (LRRRI) (2010) "Acccumulation by land dispossession and labour devaluation in Tanzania". Haki Ardhi. Available at: www.hakiardhi.org/index.php.

Lanz, K., Gerber, J.-D. and Haller, T. (2018) "Land grabbing, the state and chiefs: The politics of extending commercial agriculture in Ghana", *Development and Change; Oxford*, 49(6), pp. 1526–1552.

Lavers, T. (2012) " 'Land grab' as development strategy? The political economy of agricultural investment in Ethiopia", *The Journal of Peasant Studies*, 39(1), pp. 105–132. doi: 10.1080/03066150.2011.652091.

Lavers, T. and Boamah, F. (2016) "The impact of agricultural investments on state capacity: A comparative analysis of Ethiopia and Ghana", *Geoforum*, 72, pp. 94–103. doi: 10.1016/j.geoforum.2016.02.004.

Lemarchand, R. and Legg, K. (1972) "Political clientelism and development: A preliminary analysis", *Comparative Politics*, 4(2), pp. 149–178. doi: 10.2307/421508.

Lofchie, M. F. (2014) *The political economy of Tanzania: Decline and recovery*. Philadelphia, Pennsylvania: University of Pennsylvania Press.

Lorgen, C. C. (2000) "Villagisation in Ethiopia, Mozambique, and Tanzania", *Social Dynamics*, 26(2), pp. 171–198. doi: 10.1080/02533950008458699.

Lowndes, V. and Roberts, M. (2013) *Why institutions matter: The new institutionalism in political science.* Basingstoke, England: Palgrave Macmillan.

Lund, C. (2011) "Fragmented sovereignty: Land reform and dispossession in Laos", *The Journal of Peasant Studies*, 38(4), pp. 885–905.

Lund, C. (2013) "The past and space: On arguments in African land control", *Africa: The Journal of the International African Institute*, 83(1), pp. 14–35.

Lund, C. and Boone, C. (2013) "Introduction: Land politics in Africa – Constituting authority over territory, property and persons", *Africa*, 83(1), pp. 1–13. doi: 10.1017/S000197201200068X.

Lusasi, J., Pedersen, R. H. and Friis-Hansen, E. (2019) *A typology of domestic private land-based investors in Africa: Evidence from Tanzania's timber rush.* Working Paper 2019:4. DIIS Working Paper. Available at: https://www.econstor.eu/handle/10419/204629 (Accessed: 18 November 2019).

MAFAP (2012) "Analysis of incentives and disincentives for sugar in the United Republic of Tanzania", FAO. Available at: http://www.fao.org/3/at483e/at483e.pdf (Accessed: 2 September 2021).

Magnan, A. (2015) "The financialization of agri-food in Canada and Australia: Corporate farmland and farm ownership in the grains and oilseed sector", *Journal of Rural Studies*, 41, pp. 1–12. doi: 10.1016/j.jrurstud.2015.06.007.

Magnan, A. and Sunley, S. (2017) "Farmland investment and financialization in Saskatchewan, 2003–2014: An empirical analysis of farmland transactions", *Journal of Rural Studies*, 49, pp. 92–103. doi: 10.1016/j.jrurstud.2016.11.007.

Makki, F. (2014) "Development by dispossession: Terra Nullius and the social-ecology of new enclosures in Ethiopia", *Rural Sociology*, 79(1), pp. 79–103.

Malipula, M. (2014) "Depoliticised ethnicity in Tanzania: A structural and historical narrative", *Afrika focus*, 27(2), pp. 49–70.

Mandani, M. (1996) *Citizen and subject: Contemporary Africa and the legacy of late colonialism.* Princeton, New Jersey, United States: Princeton University Press.

Mande, M. (2010) "CCM old guard, incumbents routed in party primaries", *The East African*. Available at: https://www.theeastafrican.co.ke/news/ea/CCM-old-guard-incumbents-routed-in-party-primaries/4552908-972914-format-xhtml-kwbnenz/index.html (Accessed: 18 March 2019).

Mann, M. (1984) "The autonomous power of the state: Its origins, mechanisms and results", *European Journal of Sociology*, 25 (2), pp. 185–213. doi: 10.1017/S0003975600004239.

Margulis, M. E., McKeon, N. and Borras Jr., S. M. (2013) "Land grabbing and global governance: Critical perspectives", *Globalizations*, 10(1), pp. 1–23. doi: 10.1080/14747731.2013.764151.

Maruba, J. L. (2008) *Globalization and Africa*. Hauppauge, New York, United States: Nova Sciences Publishers.

Maruo, S. (2002) "Differentiation of subsistence farming patterns among the Haya banana growers in Northwestern Tanzania", *African Study Monograph*, 23(4), pp. 147–175.

Matandiko, K. (2017) "Tanzania: Sumaye – confiscation of my farms is a political game", *The Citizen*. Available at: http://allafrica.com/stories/201708230289.html (Accessed: 2 September 2021).

Mbashiru, K. (2016) "Tanzania: Bakhresa lands sugar covenant", *Tanzania Daily News*, 7 October. Available at: http://www.ibn-tv.co.tz/2016/10/%E2%80%8Bbakhresa-lands-sugar-covenant/ (Accessed: 2 September 2021).

Mbembe, A. (2010) *Sortir de la grande nuit: essai sur l'Afrique décolonisée*. Paris: Éditions Découverte.

Mbilinyi, M. (2016) "Analysing the history of agrarian struggles in Tanzania from a feminist perspective", *Review of African Political Economy*, 43(sup1), pp. 115–129. doi: 10.1080/03056244.2016.1219036.

McCarthy, J. F., Vel, J. A. C. and Afiff, S. (2012) "Trajectories of land acquisition and enclosure: Development schemes, virtual land grabs, and green acquisitions in Indonesia's Outer Islands", *The Journal of Peasant Studies*, 39(2), pp. 521–549. doi: 10.1080/03066150.2012.671768.

McMichael, P. (2013) "Value-chain agriculture and debt relations: Contradictory outcomes", *Third World Quarterly*, 34(4), pp. 671–690. doi: 10.1080/01436597.2013.786290.

McMichael, P. (2014) "Rethinking land grab ontology", *Rural Sociology*, 79(1), pp. 34–55.

McSweeney, K. et al. (2017) "Why do narcos invest in rural land?", *Journal of Latin American Geography*, 16(2), pp. 3–29. doi: 10.1353/lag.2017.0019.

Migdal, J. S. (1997) "Researching the state", in Lichbach, Mark Irving and Zuckerman, Alan S. (eds) *Comparative politics: Rationality, culture, and structure*. Cambridge Studies in Comparative Politics. Cambridge, England; New York, USA: Cambridge University Press (Cambridge studies in comparative politics), pp. 162–92.

Migdal, J. S. (2001) *State in society studying how states and societies transform and constitute one another*. New York: Cambridge University Press (Cambridge studies in comparative politics).

Miguel, E. (2004) "Tribe or nation?: Nation building and public goods in Kenya versus Tanzania", *World Politics*, 56(3), pp. 327–362.

Ministry of Lands, Housing and Human settlements development (2015) "Concept note: Programme for planning, surveying and land titling in Tanzania". Government of Tanzania.

Ministry of Lands, Housing and Human Settlements Development (2018) "Revised National Land Policy, 1995, Draft". Dar es Salaam, Tanzania.

Mkodzongi, G. (2016) "'I am a paramount chief, this land belongs to my ancestors': The reconfiguration of rural authority after Zimbabwe's land reforms", *Review of African Political Economy*, 43(S1), pp. 99–114.

Mmari, D. E. (2015) "The challenge of intermediary coordination in smallholder sugarcane production in Tanzania", *The Journal of Modern African Studies*, 53(1), pp. 51–68.

Mulisa, M. (2016) "Tanzania: 10,000 Kagera land developers assured of titles", *Daily News* [Preprint]. Available at: http://allafrica.com/stories/201608220831.html (Accessed: 2 September 2021).

Murray Li, T. (2011) "Centering labor in the land grab debate", *The Journal of Peasant Studies*, 38(2), pp. 281–298.

Must, E. (January 1, 2018) "Structural inequality, natural resources and mobilization in Southern Tanzania", *African Affairs,* 117(466), pp. 83–108. https://doi.org/10.1093/afraf/adx048.

Mwalimu, S. (2015) "Top Rubada officials in Sh2.6bn scandal", *The Citizen*, 9 April. Available at: http://www.thecitizen.co.tz/News/national/Top-Rubada-officials-in-scandal/1840392-2680148-cgf7l1z/index.html (Accessed: 2 September 2021).

Nalepa, R. A., Short Gianotti, A. G. and Bauer, D. M. (2017) "Marginal land and the global land rush: A spatial exploration of contested lands and state-directed development in contemporary Ethiopia", *Geoforum*, 82, pp. 237–251. doi: 10.1016/j.geoforum.2016.10.008.

Nolte, K., Chamberlain, W. and Giger, M. (2016) "International land deals for agriculture fresh insights from the land matrix: Analytical report II". Bern, Montpellier, Hamburg, Pretoria: Centre for Development and Environment, University of Bern; Centre de coopération internationale en recherche agronomique pour le développement; German Institute of Global and Area Studies; University of Pretoria; Bern Open Publishing.

Nwibo, S. U. and Okorie, A. (2013) "Constraints to entrepreneurship and investment decisions among agribusiness investors in Southeast, Nigeria", *International Journal of Small Business and Entrepreneurship Research*, 1(4), pp. 30–42.

Nyeko, O. (2021) *Tanzania: Human rights priorities for Tanzania's new president.* Human Rights Watch. Available at: https://www.hrw.org/news/2021/05/20/tanzania-human-rights-priorities-tanzanias-new-president (Accessed: 17 June 2021).

Olivier De Sardan, J.-P. (2015) "Practical norms. Informal regulations within public bureaucracies (in Africa and beyond)", in Olivier De Sardan, J.-P. and De Herdt, T. (eds) *Real governance and practical norms in Sub-Saharan Africa: The game of the rules.* London, England; New York, United States: Routledge Studies in African Politics and International Relations, pp. 19–62.

Olwig, M. F. et al. (2015) "Inverting the moral economy: The case of land acquisitions for forest plantations in Tanzania", *Third World Quarterly*, 36(12), pp. 2316–2336. doi: 10.1080/01436597.2015.1078231.

Ombuor, R. and Bearak, M. (2021) "Tanzania's Samia Suluhu Hassan acknowledged the pandemic and is promising change. Critics are unconvinced.", *The Washington Post*, 7 April. Available at: https://www.washingtonpost.com/world/2021/04/07/tanzania-samia-suluhu-coronavirus/ (Accessed: 17 June 2021).

Osabuohien, E. S. et al. (2019) "Female labor outcomes and large-scale agricultural land investments: Macro-micro evidence from Tanzania", *Land Use Policy*, 82, pp. 716–728.

Oya, C. (2012) "Contract farming in Sub-Saharan Africa: A survey of approaches, debates and issues", *Journal of Agrarian Change*, 12(1), pp. 1–33.

Pedersen, Rasmus H., and Thabit Jacob. "Political Settlement and the Politics of Legitimation in Countries Undergoing Democratisation: Insights from Tanzania." Manchester, England: Effective States and Inclusive Development Research Centre (ESID), July 2019.

Pedersen, R. H. (2016) "Access to land reconsidered: The land grab, polycentric governance and Tanzania's new wave land reform", *Geoforum*, 72, pp. 104–113. doi: 10.1016/j.geoforum.2015.12.010.

Peluso, N. L. and Lund, C. (2011) "New frontiers of land control: Introduction", *The Journal of Peasant Studies*, 38(4), pp. 667–681. doi: 10.1080/03066150.2011.607692.

Persson, A. G. M. (2019) *Foreign direct investment in large-scale agriculture in Africa: Economic, social and environmental sustainability in Ethiopia.* 1st ed., Abingdon, England; New York, United States: Routledge contemporary Africa series. doi: 10.4324/9780429020018.

Pinkney, R. (2001) *The international politics of East Africa.* Manchester, England; New York, United States: Manchester University Press.

Planning Commission (1999) "The Tanzania Development Vision 2025", Government of Tanzania.

Planning Commission, President's office (2012) "The Tanzania Five Year Development Plan 2011/12-2015/16", Government of Tanzania.

Porsani, J., Caretta, M. A. and Lehtilä, K. (2019) "Large-scale land acquisitions aggravate the feminization of poverty: Findings from a case study in Mozambique", *GeoJournal*, 84(1), pp. 215–236.

Provini, O. and Schlimmer, S. (2016) "Négocier l'action publique dans un État sous régime d'aide: une analyse comparée des politiques de l'enseignement supérieur et du foncier en Tanzanie", *Revue Internationale de Politique Comparée*, 23(2), pp. 199–223.

Purdon, M. (2013) "Land acquisitions in Tanzania: Strong sustainability, weak sustainability and the importance of comparative methods", *Journal of Agricultural and Environmental Ethics*, 26(6), pp. 1127–1156. doi: 10.1007/s10806-013-9442-2.

"Push-ups and pushback" (2016) *Africa Confidential*, 57(19). https://www.africa-confidential.com:1070/article-preview/id/11786/Push-ups_and_pushback

Rasmussen, J. and Strøh Varming, K. (2016) "Governing economies in areas of limited statehood: Anthropological perspectives". DIIS (Danish Institute for International Studies), Working Paper 4.

Reining, P. C. (1962) "Haya land tenure: Landholding and tenancy", *Anthropological Quarterly*, 35(2), pp. 58–73. doi: 10.2307/3317004.

Reuters (2017) "Tanzania's president warns journalists that press freedom has limits", *World News*, 24 March. Available at: https://www.reuters.com/article/us-tanzania-media/tanzanias-president-warns-journalists-that-press-freedom-has-limits-idUSKBN16V25S (Accessed: 10 March 2019).

Roesch, R. (2021) "Under the disguise of participation: Community forestry as a new form of land rush in Liberia", in Cochrane, L. and Andrews, N. (eds) *The transnational land rush in Africa, a decade after the spike*. Cham, Switzerland: Palgrave MacMillan (International political economy series), pp. 139–172.

Roop, S. and Weghorst, K. (2016) "The 2015 national elections in Tanzania", *Electoral Studies*, 43, pp. 190–194. doi: 10.1016/j.electstud.2016.05.003.

Rubada (2013) "Rufiji Basin Development Authority (RUBADA), Strategic Plan for the Period 2013/14—2017/18".

Schlimmer, S. (2017a) *Construire l'État par les politiques foncières. La négociation des transactions foncières en Tanzanie*. Bordeaux, France (Ph.D. thesis): Université de Bordeaux.

Schlimmer, S. (2018) "Talking 'land grabs' is talking politics: Land as politicised rhetoric during Tanzania's 2015 elections", *Journal of Eastern African Studies*, 12(1) (2 January 2018), pp. 1–19. doi: 10.1080/17531055.2017.1410757.

Schneider, L. (2004) "Freedom and unfreedom in rural development: Julius Nyererem Ujamaa Vijijini and Villagization", *Canadian Journal of African Studies / Revue Canadienne des Études Africaines*, 38(2), pp. 344–392.

Schneider, L. (2014) *Government of development: Peasants and politicians in postcolonial Tanzania*. Bloomington: Indiana University Press.

Schoneveld, G., German, L. A. and Nutakor, E. (2010) "Towards sustainable biofuel development: Assessing the local impacts of large-scale foreign land acquisitions in Ghana", in. *World Bank Land Governance Conference*, Washington, DC.

Schönweger, O. and Messerli, P. (2015) "Land acquisition, investment, and development in the lao coffee sector: Successes and failures", *Critical Asian Studies*, 47(1), pp. 94–122. doi: 10.1080/14672715.2015.997095.

Scoones, I. et al. (2019) "Narratives of scarcity: Framing the global land rush", *Geoforum*, 101(Complete), pp. 231–241. doi: 10.1016/j.geoforum.2018.06.006.

Scott, J. C. (1972) "The erosion of patron-client bonds and social change in rural Southeast Asia", *The Journal of Asian Studies*, 32(1), pp. 5–37. doi: 10.2307/2053176.

Scott, J. C. (1998) *Seeing like a state how certain schemes to improve the human condition have failed*. New Haven: Yale University Press (Yale agrarian studies).

Scott, W. R. (2001) *Institutions and organizations*. 2nd ed. Thousand Oaks: Sage Publications (Foundations for organizational science).

Sheahan, M. and Barrett, C. B. (2017) "Ten striking facts about agricultural input use in Sub-Saharan Africa", *Food Policy*, 67, pp. 12–25. doi: 10.1016/j.foodpol.2016.09.010.

Shivji, I. G. (1992) "Report of the presidential commission of inquiry into land matters/ volume 1: Land policy and Land tenure structure". The Ministry of Lands, Housing, and Urban Development, Government of Tanzania.

Shivji, I.G. (2006) "Lawyers in neoliberalism: Authority's professional supplicants or society's amateurish conscious". Valedictory lecture on Issa G. Shivji's formal retirement. Available at: http://mokoro.co.uk/land-rights-article/lawyers-in-neoliberalism-authorMB-professional-supplicants-or-societys-amateurish-conscience/ (Accessed: 15 September 2021).

Sibeon, R. (1999) "Agency, structure, and social chance as cross-disciplinary concepts", *Politics*, 19(3), pp. 125–178.

Sil, R. and Katzenstein, P. J. (2010) "Analytic eclecticism in the study of world politics: Reconfiguring problems and mechanisms across research traditions", *Perspectives on Politics*, 8(2), pp. 411–431.

Sippel, S. R., Larder, N. and Lawrence, G. (2017) "Grounding the financialization of farmland: Perspectives on financial actors as new land owners in rural Australia",

Agriculture and Human Values, 34(2), pp. 251–265. doi: 10.1007/s10460-016-9707-2.

Skarstein, R. (2005) "Economic liberalization and smallholder productivity in Tanzania. From promised success to real failure, 1985–1998", *Journal of Agrarian Change*, 5(3), pp. 334–362.

Snyder, K. A. et al. (2020) "'Modern' farming and the transformation of livelihoods in rural Tanzania", *Agriculture and Human Values; Dordrecht*, 37(1), pp. 33–46.

de Soto, H. (2000) *The mystery of capital: Why capitalism triumphs in the West and fails everywhere else.* New York: Basic Books.

Spoor, M. (2012) "Russian agroholdings + financial capital + land grabbing = Global 'Bread Basket'?" IAMO Forum 2012, Halle/ Saale, Germany, 20 June.

Stokes, Susan C. (2011) "Political Clientelism", Edited by Robert E. Goodin. *The Oxford Handbook of Political Science*, pp. 1–27. https://doi.org/10.1093/oxfordhb/9780199604456.013.0031.

Sulle, E. (2016) "Land grabbing and agricultural commercialization duality: Insights from Tanzania's transformation agenda", *Afriche orienti*, anno XVII(3), pp. 109–128.

Sulle, E. (2017) "The state of land-based investments in Tanzania: A situational analysis report". TNRF (Tanzania Natural Resource Forum).

Sulle, E. and Nelson, F. (2009) "Biofuels, land access and rural livelihoods in Tanzania". International Institute for Environment and Development.

Swantz, M-L. (1996) "'Village development: On whose conditions?'", in Swantz, M-L. and Tripp, A.M. (eds) *What went right in Tanzania: People's response to directed development.* Dar es Salaam: Dar Es Salaam University Press, pp. 137–173.

Tairo, A. (2016) "President Magufuli orders control of sugar import", *The East African*. Available at: https://www.theeastafrican.co.ke/tea/news/east-africa/president-magufuli-orders-control-of-sugar-import--1346812 (Accessed: 2 September 2021).

Tanzania Daily News (2017) "Tanzania: Escrow monster resurfaces", 20 June. Available at: https://allafrica.com/stories/201706200282.html (Accessed: 10 March 2019).

"Tanzania Parliamentary Results" (2015). National Election Commission Tanzania.

Taylor, B. (2020) "Tanzania's election results are predictable. What happens next is not". *African Arguments*, 27 October. Available at: https://africanarguments.org/2020/10/tanzania-election-results-are-predictable-what-happens-next-is-not/ (Accessed: 17 June 2021).

Theodory, T. F. (2017) "Contemporary transnational corporations' land grabs and the implications for African smallholder farmers in Tanzania", in Warikandwa, V. and Nhemachena, A. (eds) *Transnational land grabs and restitution in an age of the (De-) Militarised new scramble for Africa*. Oxford: African Books Collective, pp. 265–286.

Thomas, D. (2021) "Is Magufuli's Covid-19 response a threat to the region?", *African Business*, 9 March. Available at: https://african.business/2021/03/technology-information/magufulis-covid-19-negligence-threatens-region/ (Accessed: 17 June 2021).

Tordoff, W. (1965) "Regional administration in Tanzania", *The Journal of Modern African Studies*, 3(1), pp. 63–89.

Tripp, A. M. (1997) *Changing the rules: The politics of liberalization and the urban informal economy in Tanzania*. Berkeley: University of California Press.

Tripp, Aili Mari (2012) "Donor Assistance and Political Reform in Tanzania." Working Paper No. 2012/37. UNU-WIDER (World Institute for Development Economics Research). https://www.wider.unu.edu/publication/donor-assistance-and-political-reform-tanzania.

Tsubura, M. (2018) "'Umoja ni ushindi (Unity is victory)': Management of factionalism in the presidential nomination of Tanzania's dominant party in 2015", *Journal of Eastern African Studies*, 12(1), pp. 63–82.

Tufa, F. A., Amsalu, A. and Zoomers, E. B. (2018) "Failed promises: Governance regimes and conflict transformation related to Jatropha cultivation in Ethiopia", *Ecology and Society*, 23(4), pp. 26–37.

Ubink, J. M. (2008) *In the land of the chiefs: Customary law, land conflicts, and the role of the state in Peri-Urban Ghana*. Leiden University. Available at: http://hdl.handle.net/1887/12630.

Ubwani, Z. (2016) "Tanzania: More emerges on brutal killings", *The Citizen*. Available at: https://allafrica.com/stories/201610040725.html (Accessed: 18 March 2019).

Vercillo, S. and Hird-Younger, M. (2019) "Farmer resistance to agriculture commercialisation in northern Ghana", *Third World Quarterly*, 40(4), pp. 763–779.

Vicol, M. (2017) "Is contract farming an inclusive alternative to land grabbing? The case of potato contract farming in Maharashtra, India", *Geoforum*, 85, pp. 157–166.

Visser, O. (2015) "Finance and the global land rush: Understanding the growing role of investment funds in land deals and large-scale farming", *Canadian Food Studies / La Revue canadienne des études sur l'alimentation*, 2(2), pp. 278–286. doi: 10.15353/cfs-rcea.v2i2.122.

Visser, O., Mamonova, N. and Spoor, M. (2012) "Oligarchs, megafarms and land reserves: Understanding land grabbing in Russia", *The Journal of Peasant Studies*, 39(3–4), pp. 899–931. doi: 10.1080/03066150.2012.675574.

van de Walle, N. (2001) *African economies and the politics of permanent crisis, 1979–1999*. New York: Cambridge University Press (Political economy of institutions and decisions).

Walwa, W. J. (2017) "Land use plans in Tanzania: Repertoires of domination or solutions to rising farmer–herder conflicts?", *Journal of Eastern African Studies*, 11(3), pp. 408–424. doi: 10.1080/17531055.2017.1359878.

Washington Post (2021) "Tanzania's new leader acknowledged the pandemic and promised more civil rights. Critics are unconvinced", 7 April. Available at: https://www.washingtonpost.com/world/2021/04/07/tanzania-samia-suluhu-coronavirus/ (Accessed: 17 June 2021).

West, J. and Haug, R. (2017) "The vulnerability and resilience of smallholder inclusive agricultural investments in Tanzania", *Journal of Eastern African Studies*, 11(4), pp. 670–691. doi: 10.1080/17531055.2017.1367994.

White, B. et al. (2012) "The new enclosures: Critical perspectives on corporate land deals", *The Journal of Peasant Studies*, 39(3–4), pp. 619–647. doi: 10.1080/03066150.2012.691879.

Wittig, K. (2017) " 'C'est comme ça que cela pourrait recommencer': L'épineuse question foncière au Burundi", *Canadian Journal of African Studies / Revue Canadienne des Études Africaines*, 51(1), pp. 1–22.

Woertz, E. (2013) "The governance of Gulf agro-investments", *Globalizations*, 10(1), pp. 87–104. doi: 10.1080/14747731.2013.760932.

Wolford, W. et al. (2013) "Governing global land deals: The role of the state in the rush for land", *Development and Change*, 44(2), pp. 189–210.

World Bank (2010) "Fiche thématique Afrique Subsaharienne: Tanzanie". World Bank Publications, Washington DC.

Young, C. (1988) "The colonial state and its political legacies", in Rotchild, Donald and Chazan, Naomi (eds) *The precarious balance. State and society in Africa*, First. New York, United States: Routledge, pp. 25–66.

Young, C. (1982) *Ideology and development in Africa*. New Haven, Connecticut, United States: Yale University Press,.

Zecki, E. (1979) "La politique des villages Ujamaa en Tanzania: la fin d'un mythe", *Tiers-Monde*, 20(77), pp. 169–186.

Index

www.ingramcontent.com/pod-product-compliance
Lightning Source LLC
Chambersburg PA
CBHW050512280326
41932CB00014B/2289